MW00637988

FAKE LOVE LETTERS, FORGED TELEGRAMS,

AND PRISON ESCAPE MAPS

DESIGNING GRAPHIC PROPS

FOR FILMMAKING

ANNIE ATKINS

JEFF GOLDBLUM

July 10, 2019.

Re: FAKE LOVE LETTERS, FORGED TELEGRAMS,
AND PRISON ESCAPE MAPS.

Dear Reader:

Watching a Wes Anderson movie is a
total-body experience. From the first
frame, you immediately enter a world ripe
with fantasia, mystique, and otherworldliness
yet still remain amid objects, the palette,
and feelings of the familiar.

Annie Atkins is a master craftswoman in
this regard. Under the knowing eye of Wes,
Annie coaxes the transcendental into a
meat-and-potatoes emotional logic. Her
designs encompass the extraordinary and
ordinary but with a feel and aesthetic
all her own. Annie makes the unreal seem
hyperreal, and the real more supremely
alive and utterly magical.

Sincerely,

Jeff

INTRODUCTION

There's an archetype of storytelling known as "the herald"—
the message or messenger that kick-starts the action. Watch
a film set in the early 1900s, and the hero is handed an urgent
telegram; some centuries earlier a king throws down a scroll.
In a 1980s romantic comedy, the main character arrives home
to her apartment, laden with groceries, and presses play
on her answering machine. The herald can be a thing, or it can
be a person, like Effie Trinket in The Hunger Games, announcing
on stage that twelve-year-old Primrose will fight to the death,
or the hundreds of letters flying out of the fireplace to tell
Harry Potter that he's off to Hogwarts. Whatever form the
herald takes, its universal function is to tell the hero that,
despite their reluctance to upset the status quo, their life
is about to unimaginably change forever. Which is the point
of all drama, really, isn't it? Nobody wants to hear a story
about somebody staying safely in their comfort zone.

It could be argued that nine times out of ten, the herald
is a piece of paper. Telegrams, newspaper headlines, urgent
love letters...all these written messages inviting the protagonist to answer the call to adventure. As a graphic designer
for film, I'm biased in this assessment, what with pieces of paper
being my profession's bread and butter. In the art department,
we don't use the term "herald" (narrative devices are the
screenwriter's problem) but we do use the word "hero": a "hero
prop" being a piece that has to pass the scrutiny of the camera,
with a character all of its own. That this could be a job—a full-
time occupation, even—can sound implausible, but the role can
be neatly validated by the mention of some of cinema's most indis-
pensable graphic props: the Goonies aren't going anywhere until
they find their treasure map; Charlie doesn't get to go to the
Chocolate Factory until he unwraps his golden ticket; nobody's
saving Private Ryan until an office clerk finds herself addressing
three letters of condolence to one mother.

Graphic props can sometimes require complicated, lengthy design
processes. In The Grand Budapest Hotel, when Zero reads the

犬反対
(Anti-Dog)

ANTI-DOG

犬ゼロの
兊崎へ
(Citizens for a
Dog-Free Megasaki)

NO TO DOG

犬反対 NO DOGS

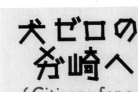
犬ゼロの
兊崎へ
(Citizens for a
Dog-Free Megasaki)

犬反対
(Anti-Dog)

うんざり?
(Fed Up?)
ゴミ島条例
賛成
(Vote Yes to
Trash Island Decree)

反犬派の学生
(Students Against Dogs)

犬 反 対

(No to Dog)

newspaper headline announcing Madame D.'s death, we had
to create an entire national press; in <u>Isle of Dogs</u> we made
enough protest banners to arm a crowd of angry people—each
of the Japanese characters fashioned with sticky tape. But
these props can also be the smallest, simplest things: if it
has any kind of lettering on it, no matter how plain the style
or how low the word count, it's usually considered "a graphic."
The now-classic business-card scene in <u>American Psycho</u> (dir. Mary
Harron, 2000) is a rare example of design making dialogue: movie
characters almost never discuss the graphics. "Picked them
up from the printer's yesterday," says Patrick Bateman, titular
psycho, throwing his new business cards onto the boardroom
table. "That's bone," he says, smugly, of the paper stock. "And
the lettering is something called Silian Rail." Bateman's composure
is shaken, though, by the apparently superior style choices
of his colleagues. His dry-throated reaction to their own cards
is wonderfully disproportionate: "Look at that subtle off-white
coloring. The tasteful thickness of it. Oh my God, it even has
a watermark...." The design of the cards—created in reality
by the movie's art department—only adds to the scene's humor,
being almost indistinguishable from one another. (Bateman's
business card was actually typeset in Garamond; Silian Rail was
an entirely fictitious font, thought up by Bret Easton Ellis,
the author of the original novel.)

In <u>Big</u> (dir. Penny Marshall, 1988), thirteen-year-old Josh Baskin
is too short to ride the roller coaster at the fairground. When he
comes across the antique fortune-telling machine Zoltar, he wishes
he were a grown-up. The genie growls, his eyes flash, and—despite
Josh noticing that Zoltar's cable isn't actually plugged in—
a small printed card shoots out of the dispenser: "Zoltar Speaks!"
On the reverse: "Your Wish is Granted." (Exit the young Josh,
who has transformed into a thirty-year-old Tom Hanks overnight,
his life now unimaginably changed forever.) The card is a hero
prop, its close-up showing off a carefully considered carnivalesque
lettering (it seems unlikely that its wording would have had the
same eerie effect had it been typeset in all-caps Helvetica).

When these small, simple things are so beautifully right for a movie,
so perfectly executed, they can seem incidental, like they must

Your Wish is Granted

ZOLTAR'S CARD (BIG)

A classic graphic prop from one of my favorite
childhood movies, this card has been kept in
pristine condition for thirty years, hidden
in a plastic folder in the basement of the movie's
set decorator, George DeTitta.

have already existed, somewhere in the fairground vernacular. Perhaps Zoltar was a real arcade machine before the film was scripted? It wasn't, although it has since become an arcade staple. The original machine, as the film's set decorators George DeTitta and Susan Bode-Tyson remember, was created especially for the movie, drawn up by the art director Speed Hopkins and manufactured by a pair of theater prop makers at a workshop in Manhattan. The box was designed to be large enough to conceal a prop man, who could hide inside and operate the genie's facial movements like a puppet, stealthily dropping the card into the dispensing slot when Josh's wish is granted. While the contact details of the two men who fabricated this piece have since been lost, it may be possible to track them down through some kind of facial recognition: they were apparently so enthusiastic about the prop, they cast one of their own faces as a mold for Zoltar's.

There is no graphic designer in the end credits of this movie, which was made in the 1980s, before the role was recognized by the United Scenic Artists union. In its most basic terms, a graphic piece could be anything that has lettering, a pattern, or a picture on it, and props like these would generally have been divided up between various members of the art department: there was usually a trainee or assistant art director who would work on graphics around their other tasks. Before art departments had computers, graphics were often drawn by hand; the impression of a professionally printed piece could be achieved with sheets of dry-transfer lettering, duplicated on the office photocopier to increase the scale. Some things were also outsourced to printers— or pieces could be begged and borrowed as they were needed. One New York set decorator recalled that as late as the 1990s, if you needed a FOR SALE sign for a character's front yard, you could just call a local realtor, jump in the car, and borrow one for an afternoon. But as scare stories about copyright lawsuits began to circulate around the industry, the role of graphic designer— someone who could produce original artwork that the production company would legally own—became almost mandatory.

It is still possible today to use real brands in a movie, of course, but now that everything has to go through a lengthy legal clearance process, it can be surprisingly more efficient—and less restrictive—

to just make stuff up. Even so, portraying a real brand in the background of a movie set can be a positive creative choice, helping to cement a story in a real time and place. This is quite different from product placement. In product placement, a film production is paid by a brand to feature their goods or artwork, which can compromise or dictate how and when the objects that dress a set are shot. Very few directors are willing to sacrifice the integrity of their story, or tolerate the disruption to their creative process, for the extra dollars. More often than not, if you see a brand you recognize in the background of a movie set, it's because the art department has requested to use their identity to create a more realistic setting for a script based on true events—or a script that wants to give the impression that it was based on true events. In Cast Away (dir. Robert Zemeckis, 2000), a delivery-service employee is stranded on a desert island after the company's cargo plane crashes in the South Pacific. While the protagonist Chuck Noland is an entirely fictitious character, his story smacks of something real, perhaps in part because the screenwriter William Broyles Jr. allegedly marooned himself on an uninhabited island during his research, but also in part because almost all the graphic design featured in the film belongs to one of the most recognizable brands in the world: FedEx.

Today, almost any movie or television series will have at least one professional graphic designer on board, sometimes as many as three or four, depending on the budget and the nature of the film's subject matter: a movie set on a farm is bound to require fewer graphics than a series set in a newsroom. While we're always focused on the director and production designer's overall vision, our day-to-day work is usually produced for the relevant department heads: magazines for the set decorator to dress into a newsstand, for example; shop-front signage for the art director to have painted onto the buildings; passports for the prop master to distribute to the actors. Graphics can then be labeled as "dressing graphics" (the pieces that decorate the sets), "construction graphics" (the pieces that are built into the sets), or "action graphics" (the pieces that the actors handle, often seen in close-up). Which graphics belong to which department can be a gray area: should wallpaper come out of the construction budget, or should it be paid for by the set decorating team? There are no fixed answers to these questions, and the workflow on every film set is different, as are the politics. (Although, it can be said that the two most important people in film design are always the production designer and the set decorator. They're the ones who win the Oscars.)

In order to create graphic pieces that feel authentic, the graphics department can enlist the help of various other crafts-people along the way: calligraphers and signwriters, bookbinders and screen printers. Digital fonts are never used in place of handwriting; prints are seldom used in place of sign painting. Researching antiquated graphic methods and styles is a large part of the design process, and much of graphic designers' prep time (the allocated weeks of work before shooting starts) is spent immersing ourselves in the period or place outlined in the screenplay. We base all our props and set pieces on real things: even the most bizarre premise for a movie has its roots in some-thing real. These pieces will most likely be developed until the source is no longer recognizable, but starting with a reference from history is what lends any graphic prop its air of authenticity.

Creating something that feels authentic is quite different from creating something realistic. While we want to be inspired by real references, we're not always stuck on realism. After The Man Who Invented Christmas (dir. Bharat Nalluri, 2017) was released, a small furor broke out online when a publicity shot showed Charles Dickens reading an alleged nineteenth-century newspaper with a large headline splashed across its front page. This was completely anachronistic, said the historians on Twitter. In the 1800s, the front page of an English broadsheet was reserved for small ads, not news stories: the Times didn't actually have headlines on its cover until the mid-1900s. But while a historian's frustration at the rewriting of the past is understandable, the work of a movie art department shouldn't be taken too literally: sometimes we just need a little artistic license. The real news stories, hidden on the inside of the paper, were always typeset to point sizes too small for any camera to pick up on in a mid-shot—and large news headlines can be an essential part of the visual storytelling process. Are we going to spend a million dollars shooting a war scene, or are we going to show a character reading a newspaper article about it instead? Headlines are a quick, effective method of giving the audience some context, and nine times out of ten, a director will forego historical accuracy when it comes to a graphic: we're telling a story, not making a documentary about nineteenth-century editorial layouts.

This isn't to say, though, that historical accuracy in graphic props can't also be used to great effect. In the first episode of the English costume drama Downton Abbey (ITV, 2010), the newspaper prop announcing the biggest story of the century—that the Titanic had sank—looks to be an exact replica of the Times of April 15, 1912, with no headline on its front cover whatsoever. The screenwriters wove this into the trajectory, with a slow reveal of the news: incorporating the delightfully peculiar tidbit that any newspapers delivered to an aristocratic country house had to be ironed by a servant. This narrative enables the second footman, William, to read the news before anyone else has a chance to set eyes on it—as he has to open the paper to iron each page individually. Consequently, the word spreads about the servants' quarters before anyone upstairs hears of it. The filmmakers have taken a moderately interesting fact about the history of English broadsheet design and weaved it seamlessly into a fascinating montage of the everyday differences between life then and life now; life upstairs versus down. "Why were the newspapers ironed?" The kitchen maid Daisy asks on our behalf: "To dry the ink, silly," she's told. "We wouldn't want his Lordship's hands to be as black as yours."

Finding a reference on which to base our designs isn't always possible. See the "incident board," for example: a real trope of set design, when a detective tacks all the clues from the latest case onto the office wall, including news clippings, mug shots of the suspects, and a map of the local area, all linked together with pins and lengths of red string. Is this how the police solve crime in real life? The reality is probably less appealing. Still, visualizing what a character is thinking is often the crux of graphic design for film, and it can call for a certain level of creativity in its execution. In Sherlock Holmes: A Game of Shadows (dir. Guy Ritchie, 2011), Dr. Watson arrives back at his old office to find that Holmes has plastered the room with clues: newspaper headlines, photographs, maps. In this case, the red strings criss-cross not just the wall but the entire room. "Do you like my spider's web?" he asks, the set an exposition of his mental well-being.

The psychological health of fictitious characters has been well documented by various movie art departments over the years: Holmes's wall is reminiscent of the paranoid schizophrenic John Nash's walls in A Beautiful Mind (dir. Ron Howard, 2001) and the CIA officer Carrie Mathison's incident board, which she builds over the course of the entire first season of Homeland (Showtime, 2011) to compile a case against the suspected traitor Sergeant Nicholas Brody. As Carrie shows signs of a potential breakdown—neglecting to take her bipolar-disorder meds and striking up a clandestine relationship with Brody—her wall becomes increasingly, visually manic, with all the classified military documents forming a rainbow timeline color-coded with bright yellow, green, red, purple, and blue. Is it mania or just genius detective work? The audience is kept guessing, finally settling on the latter just as the authorities at the CIA shut down her investigation and strip the walls of all her hard work—and the hard work of the show's graphics department. These "crazy walls"—which are almost always designed in great detail for a slow, close camera pan—take considerable effort.

In The Shining (dir. Stanley Kubrick, 1980), Jack Torrance's mental health is in question from the very earliest scenes of the movie, snowed in with his family at the Overlook Hotel as he attempts to finish his novel. It takes a graphic prop to really hammer it home, though, when his wife, Wendy, creeps toward his abandoned typewriter only to find that his entire manuscript is made up of sheer, utter madness. The varied typographic layouts of the single repeated sentence—"All work and no play makes Jack a dull boy"—indicate the final nail in the coffin. As Wendy flips through five hundred pages of superbly typed claptrap, there is no question that this is the handiwork of a madman.

Kubrick never commented on who typed the five hundred pages. Some say he did it all himself, on his programmable typewriter, setting it to repeat the lines automatically. (This wouldn't have been out of character, according to those who knew him.)

THE TIMES

THE FIRST ATOMIC BOMB

No. 50,214   LATE LONDON EDITION   LONDON TUESDAY AUGUST 7 1945   PRICE 3d

THE TIMES (LONDON, 1945)

British broadsheet newspapers didn't have news stories on the front page until the mid-1900s; the cover was, instead, reserved for small ads.

But freeze-framing the sequence reveals so many anomalies in the typing that another rumor from the set sounds more plausible: that it was the production's secretary and several other typists in the office who produced those pages for the director.

An exhibition of artwork from Kubrick's movies, most of which were found in the director's home after his death—including pages from Jack's "novel"—has toured galleries around the world since 2004. It's not uncommon for directors to hold on to hero pieces from their films (it's thought that Zoltar lived with Penny Marshall), although productions will often hold auctions to try to recoup some of a movie's budget, with pieces being bought by prop houses to be refurbished and repurposed. Occasionally, crew members might get to hold on to a piece or two that they had a hand in—I've met Cast Away's Wilson sitting on the book-shelf of the prop master, Robin Miller, and I have a couple of Mendl's boxes proudly displayed in my studio—but in the case of most graphics, the sad reality is that unless there's a real magpie of a set decorator willing to hoard drawers of these things, most pieces don't get archived. Paper has a hard time on set: the hot lights and sweaty hands of the actors quickly deteriorate graphic props, and pieces can often end up looking too distressed to be of much use as background dressing on future sets. Keepsakes might be given to the cast at times, but who knows where this stuff actually ends up: The Goonies' (dir. Richard Donner, 1985) Sean Astin is said to have brought home the now-treasured treasure map as a souvenir, only to have his mother mistake it for rubbish and throw it in the bin.

*

It can be crushing, to think of all this work being thrown away. But I'm guilty of it myself, usually preferring to clear my work-space in record time at the end of a job rather than trying to archive the piles of crumpled scraps that may or may not have made the final cut. (And who can know for sure, until we sit down in the cinema and watch the film a whole year after we wrap.) The props in the following chapters are all pieces that I've worked on for movies or shows. Not all of them are heroes, but each one was created with care, in collaboration with some of the most

wonderful and brilliant directors, designers, art directors,
set decorators, illustrators, calligraphers, and prop masters
whom I've been lucky enough to work with over the years. I hope
that looking at these graphic props close-up might shine a little
light on not just my own process, but also that of all the graphic
designers working in the film industry around the world today.
We really try to take care of all the small things, in order to help
build a much bigger picture.

CHAPTER 1

<u>DETAILS</u>

FILM SETS DON'T LOOK LIKE THE BEAUTIFULLY COMPOSED
PICTURES WE SEE ON THE CINEMA SCREEN: IN REALITY, THEY ARE
FULL OF CABLES, FLOODLIGHTS, AND CREW MEMBERS STANDING
AROUND DRINKING COFFEE OUT OF STYROFOAM CUPS. DRESSING
THIS WEIRDLY ARTIFICIAL ENVIRONMENT WITH SOME SMALL
AUTHENTIC DETAILS CAN HELP CREATE A MORE FULLY REALIZED
WORLD FOR THE DIRECTOR AND THE CAST TO WORK IN—EVEN IF
THESE PIECES ARE NEVER SEEN IN CLOSE-UP BY THE AUDIENCE.

It's hard to comprehend the level of fear that Russia's Cold War with the United States instilled in kids during the last century. Growing up in the late 1980s, I'd really only caught the tail end of it. There was some anxiety about the bomb in one of the Judy Blume books I'd read, and I'd pored over my older brother's copy of When the Wind Blows (1982), Raymond Briggs's illustrated story of a retired couple graphically dying from radiation sickness. But I read with fascination rather than with any kind of pressing worry. My parents seemed nonchalant about nuclear war: at that point it was an anxiety that had, for the most part, come and gone.

Steven Spielberg's Bridge of Spies (2015) is set in the late 1950s, and the threat of an atomic bomb being dropped on New York is a real concern—especially for the youngest son in the Donovan household, Roger, who, having seen the public-service film Duck and Cover at school, now hoards pamphlets and magazine articles on how to survive a holocaust. When his dad, James (Tom Hanks), finds him crouched on the bathroom floor with all his reading material and a tub full of emergency-use-only water, it's time for a reassuring chat. At this point, though, it's really too late: Roger has already drawn up a crayoned diagram of the bomb's reach from the center of Manhattan all the way to their doorstep in Brooklyn.

Reading a script like this felt like an unimaginable privilege. Spielberg's movies had shaped my childhood—Jaws, E.T., Raiders of the Lost Ark, Jurassic Park, along with all the other family adventure films that he had pioneered. There was no cinema in our leafy Welsh valley (this was rural Snowdonia, and the nearest large town was a fifty-mile round-trip away), but the family that lived across the lane had an enormous color television, a VCR, and a mountain of blank VHS tapes. As the eldest, it was my job to pause the recording of each movie during the ad breaks, usually leading to gaps in entire chunks of dialogue when we played them back, which we did time and time again, until the tape wore out and the films became blurred and fuzzy—although never deemed completely unwatchable, not to four little square-eyed kids. We knew the stories inside out—shouting lines from E.T. to each other up in the forest, reenacting whole scenes from Jaws down at the river—and when my mother once had to console me after a row with my father, she seemed to state the obvious: family life isn't like it is in the films you're always watching, you know. Well, no. The families in the films we watched were always being eaten by sharks or hunted by dinosaurs—although they usually came through it together, in the end. If only our little Welsh village could suffer just one meteor hit, one alien invasion, perhaps my own parents wouldn't get divorced? The absence of nuclear war in 1989 was, frankly, disappointing.

Twenty-five years later, when the production designer Adam Stockhausen sent me a draft of Bridge of Spies, I opened the script to a scene that seemed familiar: the family at the breakfast table, noisy, chaotic, but otherwise completely stable. The kids play with robots, squabble, and finish their homework, while their mother butters toast and their father reads the papers. It's the calm before the meteor. Or, in this case, the calm before their father, a white-collared insurance lawyer, signs up to defend a Russian spy of treason in the middle of the Cold War.

I had worked with Adam on two earlier films. On The Grand Budapest Hotel he'd hired me and the German film graphic designer Liliana Lambriev to make the graphic pieces for Wes Anderson's Empire of Zubrowka, throwing us head first into the beautiful, fictional Alpine land that he and Wes were creating on location in Germany. Later, he'd brought us back to his team to start graphic concepts for a sci-fi movie he was designing, set on board a spacecraft flying hundreds of years in the future.

Bridge of Spies belongs in a different world again: a true story, based on real people navigating real historical events. Adam would be re-creating midcentury New York, East and West Berlin, a U-2 fighter plane, an Alabama prison, a US army base in Pakistan, and a Moscow courtroom. Making these shifts to different times and places convincing to a cinema audience would require all kinds of period graphic design: the American billboard advertising and neon hotel signs, the Soviet propaganda, the emblem embedded into the floor of the CIA headquarters. And then there'd be the graphic pieces that are too subtle to ever really be caught properly on camera: the border visas, the smuggled pineapple

tins, the milk carton sitting on the family's breakfast table.
If it were Spielberg's action sequences that we'd played out
as children—"We're going to need a bigger boat!"—then it was
his scenes of our everyday domestic life that had us hooked
in the first place. Here was a chance, I thought as I read the
script, to make this world as real for this director as he'd
made his worlds for us as kids.

Find MORE of our exciting
GREAT BIG BOOKS by visiting
your local bookstore today!

THE GREAT BIG BOOK OF
FLYING THINGS
BY DEBORAH RICKETTS
ILLUSTRATIONS BY LILIANA LAMBRIEV

THE GREAT BIG BOOK OF
BUTTERFLIES
BY KIMBERLY KACHOUGIAN
ILLUSTRATIONS BY ANDREW BUTLER

THE GREAT BIG BOOK OF
POISONOUS PLANTS
BY PAMELA ELLINGTON
ILLUSTRATIONS BY HUGH SICOTTE

THE GREAT BIG BOOK OF
DANGEROUS JELLYFISH
BY LUCY MCGEEVER
ILLUSTRATIONS BY THOMAS SOBEL

THE GREAT BIG BOOK OF
WAR MACHINES
BY HENNING MOLEFENTER
ILLUSTRATIONS BY DAVID STEIN

THE GREAT BIG BOOK C? *of* **NEW YORK CITY**
1711 PINE ST., NEW YORK, NY

The Great Big Book of

WHEELS
AND WINGS

A GREAT BIG book of HUGE TRAINS, FAST
PLANES, and BIG TRUCKS (and some SMALL
ones too) perfect for VEHICLE-MAD BOYS.
From ENORMOUS heavy hauler dump trucks to
ZOOMING FIGHTER JETS, you'll discover the
BIGGEST and most POWERFUL winged and
wheeled machines EVER MADE by man.

BY ARTHUR W. BLATT, JR.
ILLUSTRATIONS BY JULIA O. HEYMANS

THE GREAT BIG BOOK C? *of* **NEW YORK CITY**
1711 PINE ST., NEW YORK, NY

THE GREAT BIG BOOK OF WHEELS AND WINGS
(BRIDGE OF SPIES)

When James Donovan, played by Tom Hanks, signs up to defend a Russian spy, his family's home is targeted by angry Americans, who throw a brick through the living room window. His on-screen son, Roger Donovan, was played by ten-year-old Noah Schnapp. Spielberg wanted to give the young boy a book to hold up over his head (kids were taught how to "duck and cover" in school to protect themselves if a bomb was dropped), and he requested a large compendium of vehicle illustrations that Roger could hide beneath.

We designed The Great Big Book of Wheels and Wings, a hardcover collection of planes, trains, and automobiles published by the fictional Great Big Book Company of New York City and written by the equally fictional author Arthur W. Blatt Jr. "Arthur W. Blatt is as mad about trucks as you are," reads the author's bio, "and he's been writing about wheeled and winged things since he was your age, too! He lives in New York with his wife, Hannah, and their cat, Reginald."

The Great Big Book of

WHEELS
AND WINGS

By **ARTHUR W. BLATT, Jr.**

WITH OVER
700
PICTURES

A GREAT BIG book of HUGE TRAINS, FAST PLANES, and BIG TRUCKS (and some SMALL ones too) perfect for VEHICLE-MAD BOYS. From ENORMOUS heavy hauler dump trucks to ZOOMING FIGHTER JETS, you'll discover the BIGGEST and most POWERFUL winged and wheeled machines EVER MADE by man.

AUTHOR BIOGRAPHY
Arthur W. Blatt is as mad about trucks as you are, and he's been writing about wheeled and winged things since he was your age too! He lives in New York with his wife Hannah and their cat, Reginald.

THE GREAT BIG BOOK Cº *of* **NEW YORK CITY**

WEST GERMAN FOOD PACKAGING
(BRIDGE OF SPIES) → →

Crossing the Berlin Wall remained possible throughout the Cold War, but the restrictions on the movement of East German citizens meant their access to Western products was limited. West Berliners would smuggle treats to their friends and family on the other side of the city—cans of evaporated milk, tinned peas, and boxes of sugar lumps. These props, based on a popular German brand, were never seen by the audience in the final cut of the film. Even so, the shoulder bags of the extras, who were lined up in the snow all day waiting to cross the border, were packed full of them.

Ellery's MILK

LETTERING SKETCH FOR MILK CARTON
(BRIDGE OF SPIES)

An early design for a milk carton on the Donovan
family's breakfast table, 1950s Brooklyn.

☞ IMPORTANT

This passport is NOT VALID until signed BY THE BEARER on page two. Please fill in names and addresses below.

BEARER'S ADDRESS IN THE UNITED STATES:

Name _____

Address _____

BEARER'S FOREIGN ADDRESS:

_____

_____

IN CASE OF DEATH OR ACCIDENT NOTIFY:

Name _____

Address _____

EXPIRATION AND RENEWAL

Unless limited to a shorter period, this passport Expires three years from the date of issue shown on page two. It may be renewed for an additional period not exceeding five years from the date of issue shown on passport. The renewal fee is Five Dollars. This passport MUST be presented with your renewal application. Renewal is shown by a stamp placed in the passport.

NEW PASSPORT

When this passport expires and you want a new one, this passport should be presented with your application for the New passport.

(See Other Important Information on Inside of Back Cover)

IMPORTANT INFORMATION FOR YOU

- **TRAVEL IN DISTURBED AREAS**

  If you travel in disturbed areas, you should keep in touch with the nearest American diplomatic or consular office.

- **PROLONGED RESIDENCE ABROAD**

  If you make your home or reside for a prolonged period abroad, you should register at the nearest American consulate.

- **LOSS OF NATIONALITY**

  You may lose your United States nationality by being naturalized in, or by voting in, the elections of a foreign state; by taking an oath or making a declaration of allegiance to a foreign state; or by serving in the armed forces or accepting employment under the government of a foreign state. If you are a naturalized citizen of the United States, you may lose citizenship by residing for 3 years in the country of your birth or former nationality, or by residing for 5 years in any other foreign state or states. For detailed information consult the nearest American diplomatic or consular office.

- **VIOLATION OF CONDITIONS OR RESTRICTIONS**

  If you use or attempt to use this passport in violation of the conditions or restrictions contained in it, you may lose the protection of the United States while you continue to reside abroad, and you may be liable for prosecution (Section 1544, Title 18, U. S. Code).

- **LOSS OR DESTRUCTION OF PASSPORT**

  If this passport is lost, stolen or destroyed, report full details immediately to the Passport Office, Department of State, Washington 25, D. C., or to the nearest American consulate. In an outlying possession of the United States, report to the chief executive, and to the local police authorities. In loss or destruction cases, new passports are issued only after exhaustive investigation.

- **ALTERATION OR MUTILATION OF PASSPORT**

  This passport must not be altered or mutilated in any way. You must not alter any dates; nor make any changes in your description, on the photograph, or on any other page of this passport. Alteration may make it INVALID. Only authorized officials of the United States or of foreign countries, in connection with official matters, may place stamps or make statements, notations or other additions in this passport.

U. S. GOVERNMENT PRINTING OFFICE

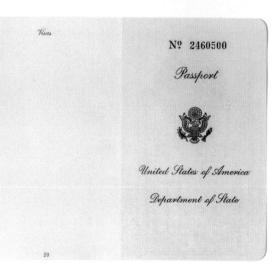

Nº 2460500

Passport

United States of America

Department of State

20

Visas

WARNING—ALTERATION OR MUTILATION OF ENTRIES IS PROHIBITED

DESCRIPTIVE DATA

NAME	JAMES BRITT DONOVAN
BIRTH DATE	FEB. 19, 1916
BIRTHPLACE	UNITED STATES OF AMERICA
HEIGHT	5 FEET 11 INCHES
EYES	BLUE
HAIR	BROWN GRAY
VISIBLE MARKS	XXX
OCCUPATION	ATTORNEY
WIFE	MARY DONOVAN
CHILDREN	JAN, JOHN, MARY ELLEN
ISSUE DATE	DEC. 20 1955

SIGNATURE OF BEARER

THIS PASSPORT IS NOT VALID UNLESS SIGNED BY THE PERSON TO WHOM IT HAS BEEN ISSUED

19

Visas

I, the undersigned, Secretary of State of the United States of America, hereby request all whom it may concern to permit safely and freely to pass, and in case of need to give all lawful aid and protection to the above-named citizen(s) of the United States.

Given under my hand and the seal of the Department of State.

Christian A. Herter

18

Photograph of bearer

Visas

4	17
6	15
8	13
10	11
12	9
14	7
16	5

No. 305651

PASSPORT

United States
of America

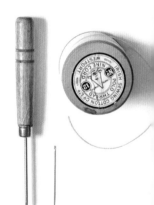

PHOTOGRAPH ATTACHED
DEPARTMENT OF STATE
PASSPORT AGENCY N.Y.

28

PASSPORT (BRIDGE OF SPIES)

Graphic prop making can feel like forgery:
James Donovan's identification started life
as a real 1950s passport, which was taken
apart, scanned, reworked, and stitched back
together again. This was a hero prop—it was
seen in close-up when the officers patrolling
the Berlin Wall asked Donovan for his papers—
but its screen time was nothing more than a
split second.

BOYS' MAGAZINE SPREAD (1950s)
(BRIDGE OF SPIES) → →

For graphic props to do their job, they would
need to really scare ten-year-old Noah Schnapp,
the actor who played Roger Donovan. We created
intentionally alarming content for the magazine articles: we wrote the pieces by imitating
the kind of inflammatory language used in real
boys' comics from the midcentury. A diagram
superimposed over an aerial shot of New York
illustrated the blast radius of "the 50 Megaton bomb." While the fireball would immediately
destroy Manhattan, its reach would go much
farther: as many as thirty miles away from
the explosion, any exposed skin would suffer
third-degree burns from the flash of light alone,
blinding anybody who turned to look at it. In
a matter of minutes, four million people across
New York would be killed. But prospects didn't
look good for those who escaped immediate
death, either. In the long term, the city would
become "a veritable wasteland, roamed only
by a few thousand desperate and terminally
ill survivors."

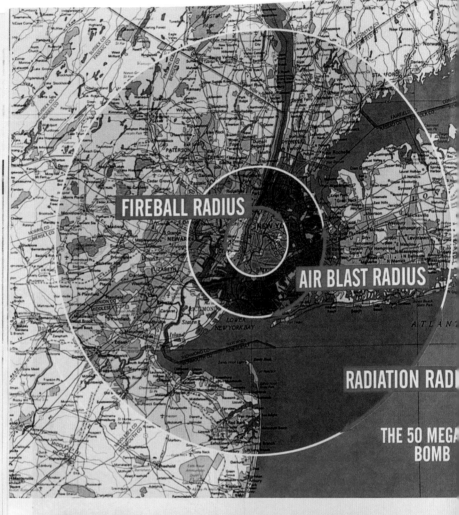

FIREBALL RADIUS

AIR BLAST RADIUS

RADIATION RADI

THE 50 MEGA
BOMB

THE BLAST RADIUS

By ARTHUR B. GORDON, Nuclear Warfare Analyst.

With the Russian advancement in both Nuclear Warfare and space patrol, "bomb" is the
hot word of the year. We asked blast analyst Arthur B. Gordon from the New York Centre for
Nuclear Research to give some examples of the effects of the 50 Megaton Bomb. Exactly how
far can we expect the destruction to reach, and what happens in its midst?

GROUND ZERO

The 50 Megaton Bomb is one of man's deadliest inventions yet, and within split seconds of its detonation a fireball explodes in every direction, reaching as far as two miles from Ground Zero and completely enveloping Manhattan Island. Temperatures would reach unfathomable heights of 20 million degrees Farenheit, vaporising absolutely everything in its path – buildings, vehicles, trees, cars, animals and people.

2-5 MILES

At two to five miles from Ground Zero this nuclear blast would produce pressures of 25lbs per square inch, and winds in excess of 650 miles per hour. The magnitude of these extreme forces would destroy everything in seconds including reinforced steel and concrete structures. Even underground bomb shelters would be crushed by the ground blasting in overhead.

5-16 MILES

At five to sixteen miles from Ground Zero the heat would melt all glass and even vaporise car sheet metal. At this distance the blast wave would create pressures of 7-10lbs per square inch and winds of 200 miles per hour.

17 MILES

At seventeen miles from Ground Zero, so strong is the heat from the fireball that just its radiant temperature alone would ignite all easily flammable materials. Curtains, paper, leaves, clothing, and gasoline would all spontaneously combust, starting thousands of fires across the land.

17-29 MILES

At distances of seventeen to twenty-nine miles from Ground Zero, the blast would still produce pressures of albs per square inch – which is enough to shatter glass windows. Shards of glass from these windows now become deadly missiles in themselves as they shoot off at 100 miles per hour.

30 MILES

At thirty miles, the heat would be so intense that any exposed skin would suffer third degree burns from the flash of light alone.

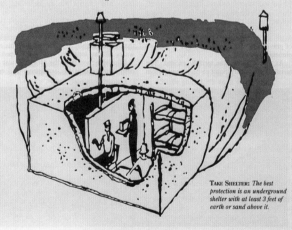

TAKE SHELTER: *The best protection is an underground shelter with at least 3 feet of earth or sand above it.*

"IF A 50 MEGATON BOMB DROPS AT THE HEART OF NEW YORK CITY, IT'S NOT JUST MANHATTAN THAT WOULD BE ANNIHILATED"

Anyone who turned to look at this sudden flash would be permanently blinded by burns on their retinas and at the back of their eyes.

100 MILES

Within a radius of 100 miles most people can expect to suffer from severe radiation sickness, beginning anywhere from half an hour to two months after the blast.

THE DEATH TOLL

Within minutes after an explosion in Manhattan, four million people across New York City would die, and more than three-quarters fatally injured. Rural and suburban New York State would suffer severe radiation sickness, and the city would become a veritable wasteland, roamed only by a few thousand desperate and terminally ill survivors.

BULLET HOLES (BRIDGE OF SPIES)

Working in different countries can present different challenges. When <u>Bridge of Spies</u>' German art director, Marco Bittner Rosser, asked me if I had "any bullet holes with me," I didn't understand what he meant. My co-graphic designer, Liliana, jumped to my rescue—she had some on her hard drive that we could use. In Berlin, the relatively large number of films produced about World War II means that most film graphic designers working locally would need to dress a location wall with fake bullet holes at some point. Photographed and printed on clear acetate, they replicate the gun damage that can still be found around the city today.

We amended Lili's files for the particular wall that would appear in the background of this shot—a long process of color-matching trial and error. On the day of the shoot, though, there was a problem that we just couldn't rectify: the freezing temperatures in Berlin in November and the thin layer of frost covering the walls meant that the acetate kept flaking off. The bullet holes were added later in post-production, instead.

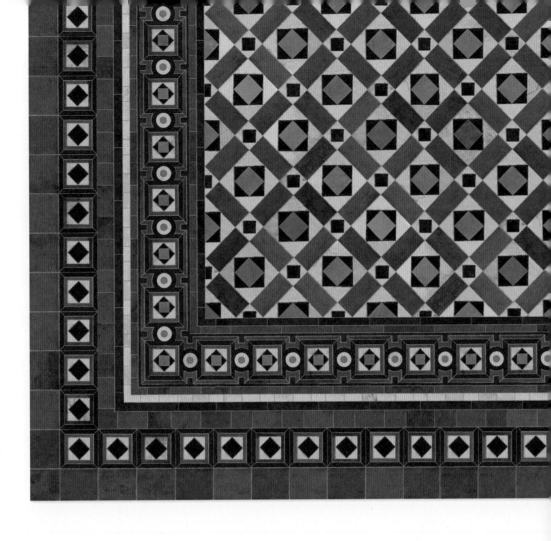

THE AMERICAN MUSEUM OF NATURAL HISTORY
FLOOR TILES (WONDERSTRUCK)

A key scene in <u>Wonderstruck</u> (dir. Todd Haynes, 2017) is set in the American Museum of Natural History, in an exhibition hall housing what was described in the script as "a cabinet of wonders": endless drawers and shelves, filled with strange and various objects—stuffed reptiles, decapitated heads, dried fish, insect skeletons, and mammal droppings. It was only the floor of this set that I would have any hand in, though: it was created digitally, and we printed over 1,200 square feet of ink on vinyl to emulate an entire tiled floor. The pattern started as flat vector artwork, and then each tile was colored and textured in Photoshop and framed with dirty grout lines to create the illusion of the tile's natural encaustic consistency.

It was important to make enough pieces and varieties so that any repeat in the texture would not be noticeable if the floor was seen at a wide angle—although the scenic artists would also add inconsistencies here and there with paint and glaze, after the vinyl had been laid. Creating flooring like this is labor intensive, and it's rare that anything more than a tiny corner of it will get a brief flash on the cinema screen. Regardless, there's something strangely satisfying about this part of the job: creating a trick of the eye, turning a flat, digital plane into something that could be mistaken as "real."

SUPPLEMENTARY COMPLAINT R...

D.D. 5 (Rev. 8-62)

Complainant's Surname | First Name

Rudolpf I.   ABEL

Complainant's Address

Room 339, Hotel Latham,

FOLLOWING QUESTIONS PERTAIN TO THIS COMPLAINT REPORT

Was this Complaint previously cleared by an arrest?
If yes, is the no additional arrest?
Were identified persons wanted previously reported?
Was any stolen property previously reported?
Was this stolen property previously reported?
Was any property recovered previously reported?
Was this recovered property previously reported?
Was complainant arrested of action taken?

NUMBER OF ARRESTS

	Male	Female	Unifor...
Adults	I	X	Detect... Other
Juveniles	I	X	Civilian

If an alarm is transmitted enter the following:

Alarm Number | Date and T...

Report of Investigating Officer:

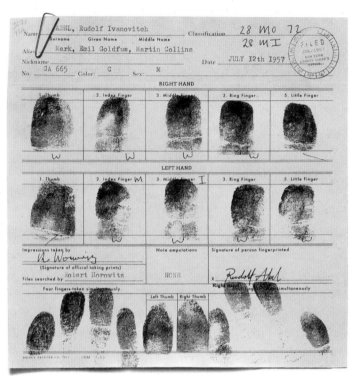

Name: ABEL, Rudolf Ivanovitch   Classification: 28 MO 72   28 MI

Surname   Given Name   Middle Name

Alias: Mark, Emil Goldfus, Martin Collins

Nickname: Date: JULY 12th 1957

No. GA 665   Color: C   Sex: M

FILED JUL-1957 NEW YORK COUNTY CLERK'S OFFICE

RIGHT HAND

1. Thumb	2. Index Finger	3. Middle Finger	3. Ring Finger	5. Little Finger

LEFT HAND

1. Thumb	2. Index Finger	3. Middle Finger	3. Ring Finger	5. Little Finger

Impressions taken by
(Signature of official taking prints)
Files searched by   Robert Horowitz

Note amputations   NONE

Signature of person fingerprinted
X   Rudolf Abel

Four fingers taken simultaneously | Left Thumb | Right Thumb | Right...

BROWN PRINTER CO 1957   10M 7-55

Союз Советских Социалистических Республик

Берлин 88
Унтер-ден-Линден д 63-65
телефон: 22 11 10

PER...

TO: DULLES; A.W.

FROM: MICHAELS; Trevor

INSTRUCTIONS: *Form must be typed or printed*

SECTION I: *All known aliases and variants (incl... data varies with the alias used, a separate form...*

SECTION II: *Cryptonym or pseudonym will be en...*

SECTION III: *To be completed in all cases.*

	SENSITIVE		201 No.	
X	NON-SENSITIVE		2892...	

NAME (Last)   (First)
DONOVAN   James   IMS...

RELATION	(Last)
W	Donovan (née McKenna)
D	Donovan
S	Donovan
D	Donovan
F	Donovan
M	Donovan (née O'Connor)

PHOTO   4. BIRTH DATE   5. COUNTRY OF...

Yale University Library

PRESENT THIS CARD WHEN BORROWING BOOKS

No. 52460

THIS CERTIFIES THAT

Frederic L. Pryor

IS ENTITLED TO DRAW BOOKS FROM:

Special student only. Room 413

and is responsible for all use made of this card. Books drawn on it
either with or without your consent must be at your risk. Loss of card
does not release you.

July 1, 1959
to
June 30, 1962

ADMINISTRATOR

No. 55/360

Subject: Abel, Rudolf charged "Espionage" –
     United States complainant.

Location: Hotel Latham,
     Room 339.

Photographer: Brown.

Taken on 7-3-57.   Eight 4 x 5 negs.

67007 4 54

**LUFTPOSTLEICHTBRIEF
AEROGRAMME**

15

VIA AIR MAIL
MIT LUFTPOST
PAR AVION

JAMES B. DONOVAN
484 Fuller Place
Brooklyn, 1 NY
United States of America

FORM 10-57   C.I.A.

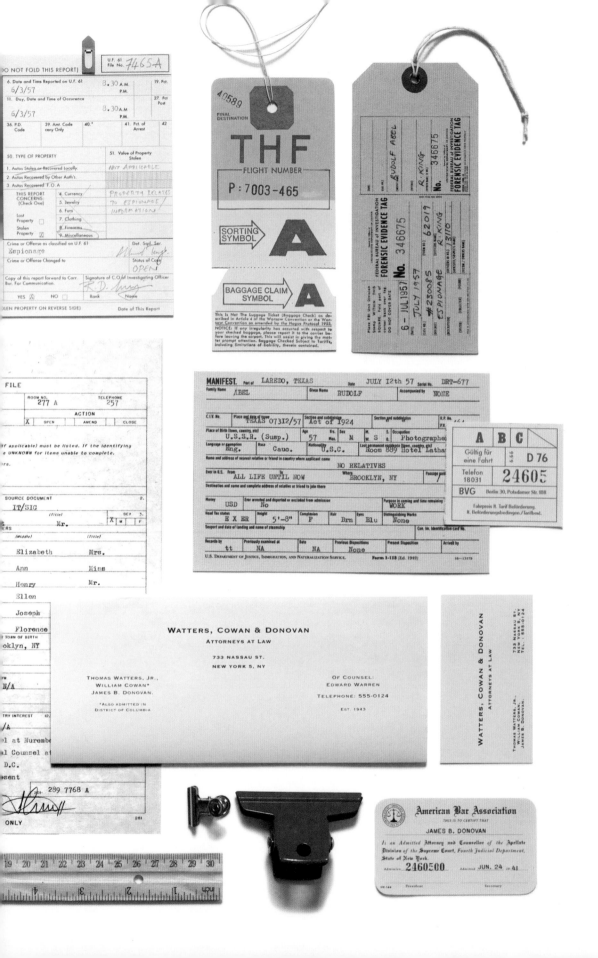

ESPIONAGE DOCUMENTS (BRIDGE OF SPIES) ← ←

Most of the graphic props created for a film aren't necessarily hero pieces but rather sheets of paperwork used as background dressing. This collection of documents was created for various scenes in <u>Bridge of Spies</u>. Although it's unlikely that much of it was ever seen in close-up, the hawkeyed prop master, Sandy Hamilton, and set decorator, Rena DeAngelo,

still pored over every detail. We used real, legible copy on the "top sheets" (the pieces that sit on the top of the stacks), actual typewritten notes, rubber stamps, and carefully selected paper types, which can all add up to create a more authentic experience for both the cast and the audience.

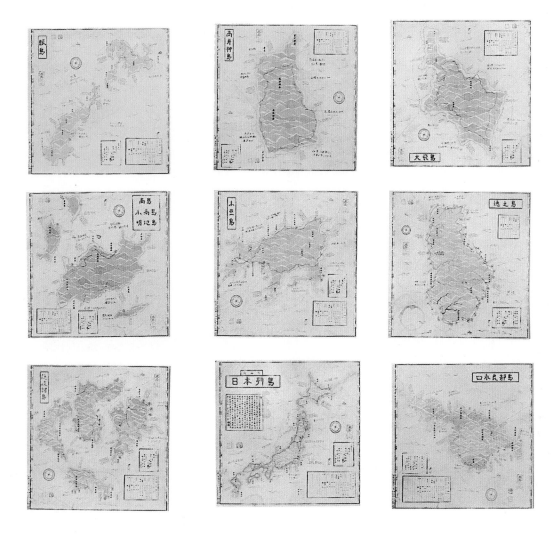

EIGHTEEN MAPS (ISLE OF DOGS)

The miniature maps on the classroom wall in Wes Anderson's Isle of Dogs depict eighteen different islands in the Japanese archipelago, each one hand drawn in pencil, marker pen, calligraphy ink, and watercolor paint. Our assistant graphic designer, Chinami Narikawa, worked closely with me on these pieces: drawing pencil outlines of Japanese island shapes while I painted textures of mountain ranges, rivers, and beaches to fill them in. As I drew the road networks and shipwrecks, Chinami would calligraph the Japanese place names and legends with a dipping pen and ink. We worked remotely, me in my studio in Dublin and Chinami in the art department in London. She would scan and email her layers to me so that I could composite them together in Photoshop. If you look carefully, you can see that some of the island shapes are the same, only flipped or rotated—although the wording and content is always right side up.

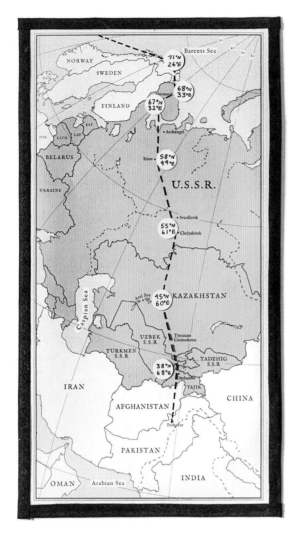

U-2 CONDENSED CHECKLIST

The following checklist is a condensed version of the aircraft checklist.

PRELIMINARY COCKPIT CHECK

☐ Seat ejection system - Check.
☐ Form 781 - Checked for aircraft status.
☐ Battery switch - Off.
☐ Autopilot controller, sextant viewing scope and driftsight control panel - Proper installation and function.
☐ Radio facility chart, appropriate letdown books - Present and current.
☐ Rubber sextant scope cover - In place.
☐ Sun shade - Securely fastened.
☐ Fan - Securely mounted.
☐ Climb data card - Installed.
☐ Under seat and behind rudder pedals - Check for loose items.
☐ Relief tube - Installed and secured.
☐ Fuel totalizer - Check.
☐ Oxygen quantity - Check for 1800 PSI minimum.
☐ Surge bleed valve sump overflow and gust control lights for night operation - Lights taped.
☐ Equipment bay upper hatch locking handles - Check.

FUEL CONSUMPTION CHART

P-31 ENGINE
NO SLIPPER TANKS

1335 GAL. TAKE-OFF FUEL
1035 GAL. TAKE-OFF FUEL

TIME AFTER TAKE-OFF - HOURS

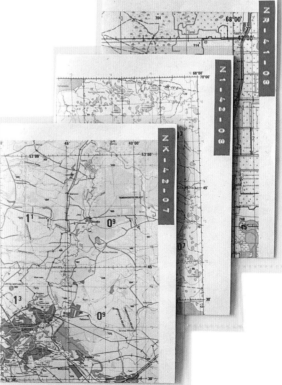

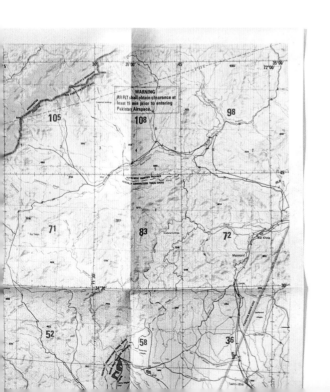

WARNING
All FLT shall obtain clearance at least 15 min prior to entering Pakistan Airspace.

U-2 PILOT COCKPIT DOCUMENTS
(BRIDGE OF SPIES)

Based on US Air Force documents from the 1950s, this checklist—known as a "green board"—was an essential part of our character's kit: it was to accompany the U-2 pilot Gary Powers on his surveillance flight over Russia. "Seat ejection system? Check." A simple map delineates the seven coordinates that would direct his route all the way from Pakistan to the most northern tip of Scandinavia. But Powers didn't complete his flight: when his plane was shot down halfway across Russia, he was forced to parachute to the ground and was captured near Sverdlovsk.

SKETCHES OF BOX LABELS
(THE BOXTROLLS) → →

Laika's stop-motion animation The Boxtrolls (2014) centers around a gang of creatures living underground, all wearing cardboard boxes for clothes. Each character is named after packaging: Shoe wears an old shoebox, Matches wears a matchbox, and Knickers's box keeps falling down. The film is gorgeously comic and imaginative, and the production designers directed us toward a loose, hand-drawn style of graphic design, stipulating that there should be no straight lines in any drawing. Instead, the line style was to vary in its weight throughout, and we wouldn't be using a font or ruler at any point in the process. The resulting artwork felt kinetic, somehow, and when the movie was finally released (stop-motion is a long process), this fundamental visual approach was a key part of the film's energy.

TWELVE DOZEN
144
EGGS
MANUFACTURED BY CHICKENS

FOR HEATERS
OIL
AND LAMPS

UNI-CYCLES
BI-CYCLES
TRI-CYCLES

CINEMA TICKETS (WONDERSTRUCK)

In Wonderstruck, twelve-year-old Rose keeps
a scrapbook dedicated to her absent mother,
a famous 1920s Hollywood actress. In addition
to newspaper and magazine clippings, the prop
master, Sandy Hamilton, asked for a page of
tickets—as if the girl had been to see every
one of her mother's silent films at the local
movie theater in Hoboken, New Jersey. While the
bright colors of the paper were based on real
tickets of the time, this would have been completely lost on the audience—the movie's scenes
set in the 1920s were shot in black and white.

The Showtime Gothic horror series Penny Dreadful (2014) was set in Victorian London but was created and shot in Ireland, with Dublin's cobblestone streets and colonial architecture doubling for London's exterior scenes as well as enormous interior sets built at Ardmore Studios in County Wicklow.

In the third episode, Vanessa (Eva Green) takes Ethan (Josh Hartnett) and Sir Malcolm (Timothy Dalton) to the zoo. It's not a day out: they go in the middle of the night, looking for Mina, Malcolm's daughter, who they suspect is a vampire. It wouldn't be possible to shoot these scenes in a real zoo—it would look too modern, for one thing, and access would be too limited. Instead, the locations department secured permission to build vintage cages in Dublin's Marlay Park, and the art directors worked with an animal handler to fill them with birds, monkeys, and a small pack of wolves. There was some talk about a tiger coming from England, too, but animal welfare regulations state that every big cat has to be transported with a mate for emotional support, which would double the cost and break the budget. Instead, the sounds of snarls and howls were added later in post-production.

In the graphics department, we designed a series of realistic zoo signage to dot the park landscape, intended to give the actors the impression of a wild animal lurking around every corner. Cast-iron directional signage featured hand-painted illustrations of zebras and bears; detailed maps of the grounds suggested exotic aviaries and a reptile house; and advertising posters promised "educated elephants" and plenty of big cats (twenty lions!). In the final cut of the episode, we see very little of this artwork, except for one blink-and-you'll-miss-it glimpse of the Monkey House information board, which is completely overshadowed by the drama unfolding next to it, as Vanessa and her gang come across what is described in the script as a "rail-thin man, not much more than a boy, hunched, devouring a dead monkey."

THE SPECIES of THE MONKEY HOUSE
OF THE ZOOLOGICAL SOCIETY of LONDON

THE OFFICIAL PAMPHLET GUIDE TO THE GARDENS IS SOLD AT THE TICKET OFFICE BY THE MAIN ENTRANCE IF YOU FIND IT SUITABLE, OR IF NOT, THE SUPERINTENDENT B.J. HARTNETT, MAY HELP.

ANY LADY OR GENTLEMAN IS ELIGIBLE FOR ELECTION TO THE SOCIETY. ADMISSION FEE £5; ANNUAL SUBSCRIPTION £3, OR LIFE SUBSCRIPTION OF £30 IN LIEU THEREOF.

Nº 1 — THE COMMON MACAQUE
Macaca cynomolgus

The Common Macaque is a native of India, and can be seen in almost every Zoological Garden in Europe.

Nº 2 — THE VERVET MONKEY
Cercopithecus pygerythrus

Vervet Monkeys belongs to the common African genus, Cercopithecus. It is mischievous and occasionally can be dangerous to humans and smaller species of monkey. The Vervet Monkey initiates fights within his own species too. The Diana Monkey and the Mona Monkey, other species of the same genus, are very handsome and more easily tamed so as to be kept as docile pets.

Nº 3 — THE SQUIRREL MONKEYS
Saimiri

The Squirrel Monkeys are long limbed, elegant creatures with prehensile tails. They enjoy jumping from tree branch to tree branch and swinging from great heights.

Nº 4 — THE CHIMPANZEE
Anthropithecus

Chimpanzees are quite intelligent, and several of them, like 'Sally' (fig. 2) who lived for many years in these Gardens, have been trained to perform tasks which show their ability to memorise and deduce problems similar to men. They show intelligence far superior to most of their species and other creatures within the Animal Kingdom. 'Sally' has lived in these Gardens for fourteen years and can quickly solve many puzzles.

Nº 5 — THE CAPUCHIN
Cebus

Capuchins are very strong and easily recognisable. Most of them have a prehensile tail, which acts as a fifth limb when climbing. They also have more teeth than other species. They use these extra teeth to grind tough nuts and shells. These little monkeys are tame and well behaved.

Nº 6 — THE WOOLLY MONKEYS
Lagothrix

The Woolly Monkeys are covered in a thicker fur, closer to that of wool, than other monkeys. They use their prehensile tail to swing from tree branches. Their are regularly persecuted for their edible flesh and warm fur.

Nº 7 — THE LION MARMOSET
Callitrichidae

Marmosets are closely related to Old World Monkeys and are well known as peaceful and loving pets. Marmosets need particular care in captivity and they diet on seed worms and fresh fruit. Marmosets are found in the Monkey House where the temperature is warmer although they spend some time socialising in the Outdoor Monkey enclosure between 9 and 10 a.m. daily. They are gentle and affectionate creatures and enjoy human interaction, making great connections with the keepers and visitors to the Gardens. They have long tails, large powerful eyes and are covered in long-haired fur.

fig. 2
THE CHIMPANZEE
Anthropithecus

PRINTED BY J. ATKINS & CO., SOUTHGATE, LONDON, BY ORDER OF THE ZOOLOGICAL SOCIETY OF LONDON. BY APPOINTMENT TO HER THE QUEEN.

THE GARDENS of THE ZOOLOGICAL SOCIETY of LONDON

PLAN OF THE GARDENS
1:28,640

Nº 13 — THE CARNIVORA HOUSE

Nº 14 — THE PARADISE HOUSE

Nº 48 — THE REPTILE HOUSE

Nº 35 — THE MONKEY HOUSE

Nº 8 — THE ZEBRA HOUSE

Nº 11 — THE ELEPHANT HOUSE

Nº		Nº		Nº		Nº		Nº		Nº	
01.	PHEASANTRY	09.	GAZELLES	17.	OUTDOOR MONKEYS	25.	OTTERS	33.	SMALL BIRDS	41.	APES HOUSE
02.	OWLS AVIARY	10.	CHAMOIS	18.	PELICANS	26.	JACKALS	34.	W. PHEASANTRY	42.	STORKS
03.	CRANES PADDOCKS	11.	ELEPHANTS	19.	EASTERN AVIARY	27.	EAGLES	35.	MONKEY HOUSE	43.	CRANES
04.	INSECT HOUSE	12.	RHINOCEROS	20.	PAVILION POND	28.	FOXES	36.	RODENTS	44.	OSTRICHES
05.	DEER YARD	13.	PARROTS	21.	GREAT AVIARY	29.	RACOONS	37.	SOUTHERN AVIARY	45.	CARNIVORA HOUSE
06.	ZEBRAS	14.	BRUSH TURKEYS	22.	SHEEP YARD	30.	DIVING BIRDS	38.	POLAR BEARS	46.	GNUS
07.	HIPPOPOTAMI	15.	KANGAROOS	23.	LLAMAS	31.	CAMEL HOUSE	39.	SWINE	47.	WOLVES DEN
08.	GIRAFFES	16.	PARADISE HOUSE	24.	MAMMAL'S CAGES	32.	BEARS	40.	SEA LIONS POND	48.	REPTILE HOUSE

PRINTED BY J. ATKINS & CO., SOUTHGATE, LONDON, BY ORDER OF THE ZOOLOGICAL SOCIETY OF LONDON. BY APPOINTMENT TO HER THE QUEEN.

№ 48

REPTILE
HOUSE

PACHYDERMS

| Elephants | Rhinoceroses | Tapirs |
| Aardvarks | Wild Boars | Hippopotami |

ELEPHANT
HOUSE

CARNIVORA
HOUSE

MONKEY
HOUSE

THE SPECIES OF THE
NEW PHEASANTRY
OF THE ZOOLOGICAL SOCIETY OF LONDON

THE SPECIES OF THE
MONKEY HOUSE
OF THE ZOOLOGICAL SOCIETY OF LONDON

THE SPECIES of THE
CARNIVORA HOUSE
OF THE ZOOLOGICAL SOCIETY OF LONDON

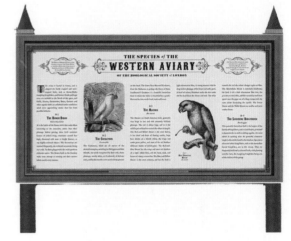

THE SPECIES of THE
WESTERN AVIARY
OF THE ZOOLOGICAL SOCIETY OF LONDON

№ 45
CARNIVORA HOUSE

№ 34
MONKEY HOUSE

№ 19
NEW AVIARY

№ 9
PEACOCK ENCLOSURE

KEEP HANDS AWAY FROM CAGE.

Please Do Not Encourage the Monkeys.

Animals Fed Daily at Noon.

PLEASE DO NOT FEED THE BIRDS.

CHAPTER 2

<u>RESEARCH</u>

IT'S EASY TO IMAGINE THE PAST AS A SEPIA-TONED PHOTOGRAPH:
MONOTONE STREET SCENES, GHOSTLY FIGURES IN FORMAL WEAR,
AND SERIF FONTS EVERYWHERE. IT'S WRONG, OF COURSE—
A COPY OF A COPY OF A COPY, UNTIL IT BECOMES A CLICHÉ.
WHEN WE DO OUR RESEARCH, THE REALITY CAN BE SURPRISING,
AND SOMETIMES MUCH MORE INTERESTING.

There was a life-drawing teacher in my first year of art school who would drum into us that we should all stop looking at our hands and our pencils and start looking at the life in front of us instead. The teacher was the Welsh landscape artist Peter Prendergast, and the life in front of us was Jan, who sat naked for us every Wednesday morning in the cold atrium of our small Welsh art college. Life drawing didn't come easily to me, and I battled with figurative art for all of my foundation year before graduating to Ravensbourne College of Design in London, where I specialized in visual communication. This did come easily—at least, comparatively easily: arranging type on a page felt much more logical than trying to depict the complete human form with a stick of charcoal. But still, Peter's principle—"Don't look at the paper, look at the world around you"—stayed with me through my studies, into a short career in advertising, and for all my design work in film.

The research stage is the first step of a film's design process, and in the early days of any production, we collect hundreds of reference images to use as the basis of our props and set pieces. Even if we end up designing a piece digitally using Illustrator or Photoshop, we still need to understand the form and context of the original in order to make it feel authentic. How does print from a letterpress printer differ from that of an engraver? How does the printing method affect the style of the lettering? It's only after we closely examine the primary source that we can imitate it convincingly.

Using internet search engines to find source material can be a wild goose chase. All the beautifully ornate Italian chocolate wrappers might have been catalogued by one careful blogger, but cheaply printed old ticket stubs don't necessarily exist in one place. Scans can be labeled incorrectly, dates are vague, and dimensions are usually missing. And even when pieces are properly archived, looking at pictures of printed ephemera on library websites can be misleading: it's not really possible to judge the scale of an old banknote, for example, in a photograph on a screen. Weights of various papers disappear in scans, textures aren't always visible, and you're never quite sure what might be printed on the back of any given piece. The "white fiver"—the black-and-white British five-pound note issued in the late 1700s—is a good example: it is completely blank on one side, but you wouldn't know this unless you held one in your hands. Nobody ever scans and uploads the blank back of anything.

Hunting for scraps of graphic design in the real world gets better results. Vintage cinema stubs, shopping receipts, postcards— all used at some point by somebody, somewhere, as makeshift bookmarks—can usually be found between the pages of any old novel. Junk shops might stock cabinets of old cigarette boxes or offer an empty vial of poison for sale. Here in Dublin, we're better off searching our grandmother's attic than expecting to find these things in antiques shops, but Germany seems to have a different relationship to printed ephemera.

In the very early days of <u>The Grand Budapest Hotel</u>, when the crew was still stationed at Studio Babelsberg, I trawled a Berlin flea market one weekend with Robin Miller, the prop master. While he hunted for treasures—spectacles, watches, ashtrays, wallets— I searched for trash, and found that all sorts of paper rubbish could be traded for cold hard cash: used train tickets, canned food labels, old passports belonging to long-dead strangers. In a crate full of old books at a market on Arkonaplatz, I found my own treasure: a 1920s diary that had belonged to a German girl, who had used the journal to collect pages of poems and well-wishes, all handwritten by various friends and relations. Why was she collecting these writings? Was she moving away? Sick? Dying? I try not to get too sentimental about these things: her diary is now my go-to reference manual for all the varied cursive handwriting styles of the early twentieth century. You just couldn't get a result like this using Google image search.

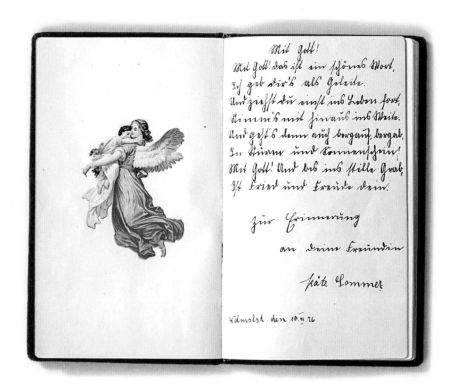

POESIEALBUM → →

A collection of poems and well-wishes written
in the journal of a German girl in the 1920s.

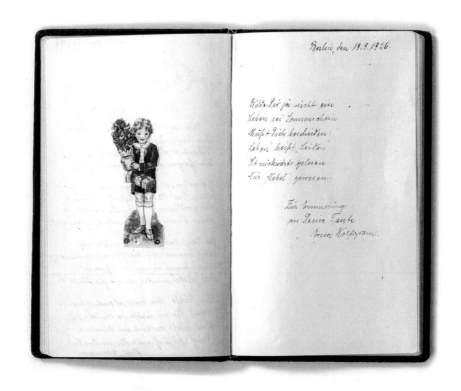

Berlin, den 19.2.1926.

Bilde Dir ja nicht ein
Leben sei Sonnenschein
Mußt Dich bescheiden:
Leben heißt Leisten
Ist rückwärts gelesen
Nur Nebel gewesen.

Zur Erinnerung
an Deine Tante
Anna Wolfgram.

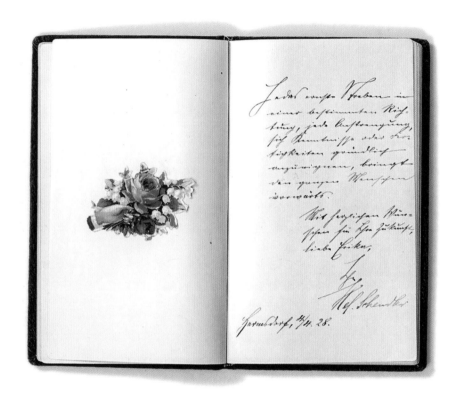

Jedes ernste Streben in
einer bestimmten Rich-
tung, jede Anstrengung,
sich Kenntnisse oder Fer-
tigkeiten gründlich
anzueignen, bringt
den ganzen Menschen
vorwärts.

Mit herzlichen Wün-
schen für Ihre Zukunft,
liebe Erika,

Ihr
Alfr. Schenker

Harmsdorf, 4/4. 28.

Der Mensch sei niedrig oder groß,
Mühseligkeit ist aller Loos.
Nicht Gold gibt Glück nicht Rang nicht Pracht,
Wir sind wozu das Herz uns macht.

Zur frdl. Erinnerung
an
Ingeborg Marchy.

Köln, den 21. VI. 1926.

PRINTED EPHEMERA

References for vintage lettering design can show up on the strangest objects. Scouring flea markets, antiques shops, and your grandmother's attic might offer up more interesting results than keying search terms into Google.

WHITE FIVER FRONT AND BACK

Britain's first five-pound note was issued in 1793. Nicknamed the "white fiver," the note was in circulation for more than 150 years, not replaced with the modern fiver until 1957. Printed beautifully and simply with black ink on white paper, at 12 × 19.5 cm (4.7 × 7.7 in.) the banknote was much bigger than today's equivalent of 7 × 13.5 cm (2.8 × 5.3 in.).

When you hold one in your hands, the biggest design surprise is that there's nothing printed on the reverse—impossible to know when you're looking at a scan of the printed side of the note online. Still, some set decorators prefer to use double-sided notes in films: even when it's accurate historically, a blank back can sometimes look a bit too "proppy."

GOODS INVOICE: FABRIC DYING COMPANY
(MANCHESTER, ENGLAND, 1936) → →

Even the most ordinary office documents can be surprisingly beautiful resources for imitating paperwork from a predigital time. This invoice from a fabric dyer in Manchester shows at least six different printing methods, including an elaborate copperplate engraving of its factory's smoking chimneys. (Clearly, something to have been proud of, in 1930s Northern England.) Pieces like these provide invaluable inspiration for methods in making any paper prop feel more finished: rubber-stamped dates, pencil signatures, two different pens, typewritten notes, and even the holes punched into the paper for binding are a different size than the ones we're familiar with today.

The red lines were the product of the Shaw Pen Ruling Machine, a large wooden and brass loom operated by two people at a time, "automatically" drawing lines onto pages that were then bound into ledgers and copybooks. Multiple pens were set at different points across a bar at the front of the machine, with ink-saturated cloths positioned just above, dripping ink onto sheets as they were fed through the machine. This process would need to be repeated up to four times, depending on the specific pattern of the lines designed for the sheet. The machine printed about one thousand sheets every half hour: a huge improvement on earlier methods, which typically involved drawing each line by hand with a ruler and a red pen.

57

1)
The words "telegraphic cypher address" are so antiquated that they now sound futuristic.

2)
Abbreviations include "Messrs" (plural of "Mister") and "Bot. of" (short for "bought of"—i.e., you bought your goods here).

3)
Company names were typically the last names of co-owners connected with an ampersand.

4)
The majority of the lettering was hand drawn and plate printed rather than set using typefaces, a distinction that can be identified by the slightly irregular spacing and sizing of the lettering: no two letters are exactly the same.

5)
The letterhead design is created with an elaborate copperplate engraving full of illustration and decorative filigree—it was typical of the time to include a depiction of the company building on its stationery.

6)
The binding holes, pierced by hand with a needle, are different in size than those punched with the modern hand-held tool we know today.

7)
These red lines were printed by a pen-ruling machine, a large industrial piece of equipment commonly used to print lines in ledgers and copybooks.

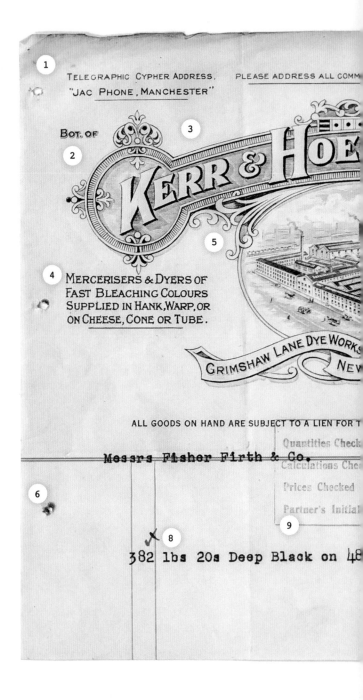

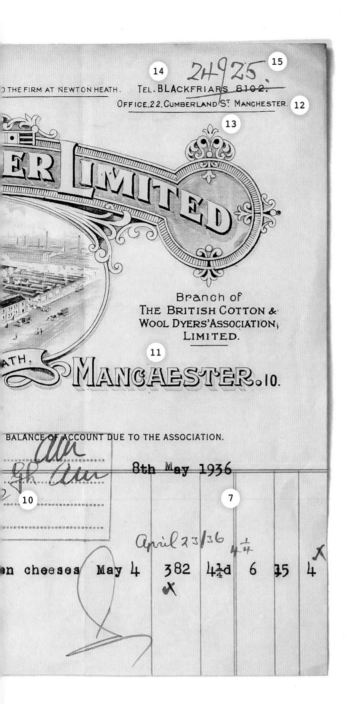

THE FIRM AT NEWTON HEATH.
14 TEL. BLACKFRIARS 8102.
2H925. 15
OFFICE, 22, CUMBERLAND ST. MANCHESTER. 12

ER LIMITED

13

Branch of
THE BRITISH COTTON &
WOOL DYERS' ASSOCIATION,
LIMITED.

ATH, MANCHESTER. 10.
11

BALANCE OF ACCOUNT DUE TO THE ASSOCIATION.

8th May 1936

10   7

April 23/36 4¼

n cheeses   May 4   382   4¼d   6   15   4

15)
Midcentury telephone numbers now seem implausibly short.

14)
Note that the first three letters of "Blackfriars" are slightly larger than the rest: commonly understood as the telephone area code.

13)
The superscript "T" in the abbreviation of "street" is positioned directly above the full stop rather than beside it—often seen in hand-lettered addresses at the time.

12)
Full stops at the end of stand-alone phrases were once common and have since been phased out.

11)
A nice embellishment by the lettering artist is the double cross-barred "H" in "Manchester."

10)
The handwriting in two different pens and a pencil suggests that the invoice had passed through many different hands.

8)
Typewritten notes add information specific to this invoice.

9)
All invoices were certified with an inked rubber stamp.

SELECTION OF OBSERVER POCKET BOOKS
(ENGLAND, 1937–c. 1960)

Books are an integral part of any research process, as authors, editors, and editorial assistants have already fact checked the text—which can make certain online resources seem like they're largely operated by cats. Books of collected printed ephemera will usually publish the dimensions of the pieces too, which is useful when you're trying to re-create a document that you can't get your hands on, and will always credit sources, which is useful when trying to secure permission for reproductions.

These Observer Pocket Books were published between 1937 and 2003 as quick go-to guides and cover all kinds of topics. They now cost anywhere from less than a dollar to hundreds of dollars each, depending on their rarity and condition. The orientation of the titles differs on the spines of the pocket books. Today, there is regional conformity: American, British, and Irish spines, for example, read from top to bottom, while German and French books read from bottom to top. This was standardized in the United Kingdom in the mid-twentieth century—and the spine-text orientation of these pocket books followed suit. Proponents of the top-to-bottom positioning thought that the spine could be read more easily when the book is laid flat on the table, whereas in Germany, France, and other countries it's believed that when the book is standing vertically on a shelf, the title is generally more readable from bottom to top. Either way, this small detail is something we have to bear in mind when we're making fake dust jackets for dressing a bookshelf on a film set. The research process doesn't have to be much more complicated than picking up a real book and taking a look at it rather than closing our eyes and just making something up.

POST ✠ OFFICE TELEGRAM

Charges to pay
_____ s. _____ d.

RECEIVED

No. _____

OFFICE STAMP.

Prefix. Time handed in. Office of Origin and Service Instructions. Words.

52

From _____

352 2.25 INVERNESS 18

T|S

MACGLASHAN AVERAGE HOTEL LANCASTER GATE LONDON-W 2 =

= SORRY MISS YOU LAST NIGHT HOPE YOURE TELLING PEOPLE

WERE ENGAGED DARLING + 2 +

For free repetition of doubtful words telephone "TELEGRAMS ENQUIRY" or call, with this form at office of delivery. Other enquiries should be accompanied by this form and, if possible, the envelope.

B or C
C

TELEGRAM (ENGLAND, 1941)

The folders of archival material I've collected over the years are a mishmash of periods and places, used as reference for shows set in places like Tudor England, Victorian London, or Communist East Berlin. I store them on my bookshelves in box files, separated by decade—or, for the older documents, by century—as well as in piles of as-yet-uncategorized (one day!) photograph albums.

Some of these pieces are more interesting than others. Deeds written with an inked quill on vellum, a colorful collection of cardboard milk-bottle tops, and—my personal favorite—a telegraphed message to someone in 1940s London: "Hope youre telling people were engaged darling." (The relationship is clearly doomed.)

MILK-BOTTLE TOPS (ENGLAND, 1950s)

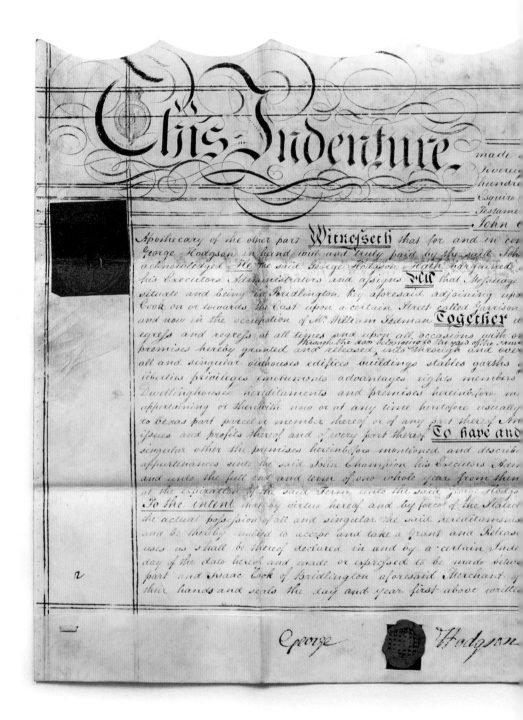

This Indenture

made ...
... Soverei...
... hundre...
... Esquire ...
... Testame...
... John ...

Apothecary of the other part **Witnesseth** that for and in cer...
George Hodgson in hand will and truly paid by the said John ...
acknowledged **He** the said George Hodgson Hath bargained ...
his Executors Administrators and assigns **All** that Messuage ...
situate and being in Bridlington Key aforesaid adjoining upo...
Cook on or towards the East upon a certain Street called Garrison ...
and now in the occupation of Mr William Seaman **Together** w...
egress and regress at all times and upon all occasions with or ...
through the soar belonging to the yard of the same
premises hereby granted and released, into the yard and over ...
all and singular outhouses edifices buildings stables garths ...
liberties privileges emoluments advantages rights members ...
Dwellinghouse hereditaments and premises hereinbefore m...
appertaining or therewith now or at any time heretofore usually ...
to be as part parcel or member thereof or of any part thereof An...
issues and profits thereof and of every part thereof **To have and** ...
singular other the premises hereinbefore mentioned and describ...
appurtenances unto the said John Champion his Executors Ann ...
and unto the full end and term of one whole year from then ...
at the expiration of the said Term unto the said John Hodgso...
To the intent that by virtue hereof and by force of the Statut...
the actual possession of all and singular the said hereditaments ...
and be thereby enabled to accept and take a Grant and Release ...
uses as shall be thereof declared in and by a certain Inde...
day of the date hereof and made or expressed to be made betwe...
part and Isaac Cook of Bridlington aforesaid Merchant y ...
their hands and seals the day and year first above written

George   Hodgson

...ourteenth ... day of September in the Fifty third year of the reign of our ... King George the third and in the year of our Lord One thousand eight ...thirteen **Between** George Hodgson of Bridlington in the County of York ... Son and heir at Law and also a devisee in fee named in the last Will and ... ...in Hodgson late of Bridlington aforesaid Merchant deceased) of the one part and ...ion of Bridlington Key in the Parish of Bridlington aforesaid Surgeon and ... ...ion of the Sum of Five Shillings of lawful money of Great Britain to the said ... ...pion at or before the sealing and delivery hereof the receipt whereof is hereby ... ...ed and by these presents **Doth** bargain and sell unto the said John Champion ... ...ts or Dwellinghouse with the outbuildings yard and appurtenances thereunto belonging ... ...n yard on or towards the North upon a Dwellinghouse house and premises of Mr John ... ...n or towards the West and upon a Walk called the Parade on or towards the South ... ...use of the Well in the said open yard **And also** full and free liberty of ingress ... ...t Horses for the owners and occupiers of the said Messuage or Dwellinghouse and ... ...open yard to and from the said Street called Garrison Street **Together** with ... ... cisterns pumps pipes of Wood or Lead ways easements waters watercourses ... ...aments and appurtenances whatsoever to the said Messuage Tenement or ... ... and intended to be hereby bargained and sold ... belonging or in any wise ... ...occupied possessed or enjoyed or accepted reputed deemed taken or known ... ...version and Reversions Remainder and Remainders yearly and other rents ... ...d the said Messuage Tenement or Dwellinghouse hereditaments and all and ... ...ereby bargained and sold or intended so to be with their and every of their ... ...rs and assigns from the day next before the day of the date hereof for and during ... ...ensuing and fully to be compleat and ... **Yielding and paying** therefore ... ...rs or assigns the rent of one pepper corn if the same shall be lawfully demanded ... ...for transferring of uses into possession the said John Champion may be in ... ...remises hereby bargained and sold or intended so to be with the appurtenances ... ...Reversion freehold and Inheritance thereof to him and his heirs To such ... ...Release already prepared and intended to bear date the day next after the ... ...said George Hodgson of the first part the said John Champion of the second ... ...rd part **In Witness** whereof the said parties to these presents have set ...

CHALLENGE: A HANDWRITTEN MANUSCRIPT
BY VITA SACKVILLE-WEST

Virginia Woolf's relationship with the writer Vita Sackville-West is well documented: more than five hundred of their love letters were published in the book The Letters of Vita Sackville-West to Virginia Woolf (2001). This was the original source material for the film Vita & Virginia (dir. Chanya Button, 2019), made in Ireland, with various locations doubling for the London townhouses and English stately homes that the two writers occupied in the twenties and thirties.

The film was meant to be graphics-heavy: both main characters are writers with "rooms of their own," and, in Woolf's case, an entire publishing house: she founded the Hogarth Press in 1917 with her husband, Leonard. Printing was originally a hobby of the Woolfs: they set up their first press in their dining room, with Virginia using the hand printing of books as a therapeutic distraction from writing. By 1946 the Hogarth Press, now on London's Tavistock Square, had published 527 titles, including three by Sackville-West.

Most of the film's interior sets would need to be dressed, then, with piles of letters, books, and manuscripts. We were lucky, in the early days of researching the artwork for the movie, to come across the Dobkin Family Collection of Feminism in New York. The archivists there were infinitely helpful, supplying us with scans of Sackville-West's personal documents, including Challenge as a working manuscript (often handwritten) rather than a publisher's draft (usually typed).

Seeing a manuscript like this is a good example of how invaluable the research process is in creating pieces that feel human: it would have been easy to conjure up a black-and-white typed document for the character, but Vita's real handwriting, with its bright red block-shadow lettering, reminds me of the textbooks that students doodle all over when they're supposed to be concentrating in school. Sackville-West was a brilliant, poetic author, but she was also consumed by self-doubt. The film shone a light on the challenges facing women writers at the time, and it was a real education to research the life and loves of Virginia Woolf rather than the more often-told story of her eventual, horribly sad suicide.

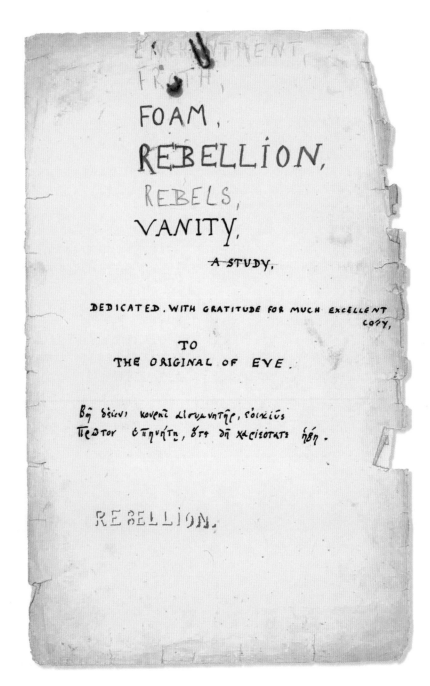

ENCHANTMENT,
FROTH,
FOAM,
REBELLION,
REBELS,
VANITY,

A STUDY,

DEDICATED, WITH GRATITUDE FOR MUCH EXCELLENT
COPY,

TO
THE ORIGINAL OF EVE.

Βῆ δ᾽ ἀκέων κονέῃ διογενῆς, εὐοικιύς
Πεδίον ὀπηνῆτε, ὅττ δῆ κλεϊστατε ἤδη.

REBELLION.

"Stormy Weather"
Lena Horne, Bill Robinson,
Cab Calloway & his Band,
Fats Waller, the Nicholas Brothers.

with Frank Fellows of Highgate
and Stan Norman of Ealing
on 5/2/44.

VENDREDI   SOIREE 9.30

CINÉMA ROYAL

Faut. de Balcon   P.T. 7   9
Taxe Gouvernementale .... » 1,5
Taxe de Bienfaisance .... » 0,5

Nº 19920 | Tout billet détaché n'est pas remboursable

CINEMA TICKETS (CAIRO, EGYPT, EARLY 1940s)

My ephemera collection as a whole isn't a particularly beautiful one to look at—more like a collection of everyday throwaway scraps that might inform a prop or two at some point. These cinema tickets from 1940s Cairo are pretty standard layouts for stubs at the time: the theater's name, date, seat number, and price are all printed and stamped, but not the movie's title. The woman they belonged to, though, had carefully written the name of the film on the back of each one, along with a note about whom she went to the pictures with on that particular day: with Frank Fellows of Highgate to Andy Hardy's Double Life and with Fellows and Stan Norman of Ealing to Stormy Weather. It's fun to feel like you're holding a tiny slice of someone's life in your hands, but this is also good reference material to answer every set decorator's question: what are you going to put on the back of this thing? While the front of a movie prop is always designed with great care, when the actor holds it up to the camera to examine it, often it's the back of a graphic that actually gets seen.

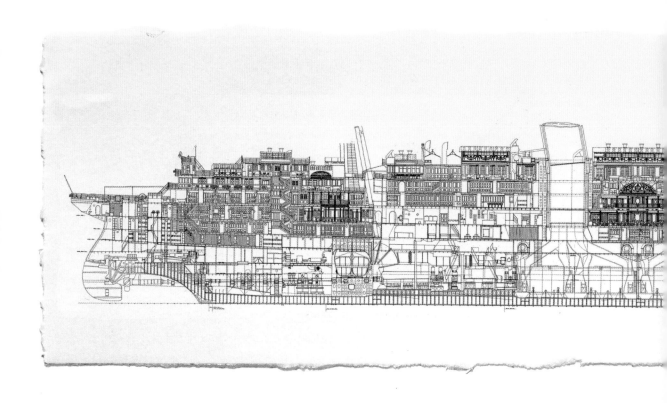

R.M.S. "TITANIC".
GENERAL ARRANGEMENT (AS FITTED)
PROFILE FORWARD.
SCALE—⅛INCH ONE FOOT.

THE RMS TITANIC WITH FOUR WORKING FUNNELS ← ←

Set in early 1900s Belfast, the television series Titanic: Blood and Steel (2012) deals with the ship's construction rather than the iceberg. One of the show's main sets was the Harland & Wolff shipbuilder's drawing office; a significant part of my role was to provide the actors playing the draftsmen with half-finished plans of the ship, which they would be working on at their desks.

In cases like this, it is futile to try to draw up brand new plans. We only had five weeks to create what would have taken a large team of expert draftsmen months upon months of work, and it was more feasible to seek permission to use the real drawings. The copyright owners, however, weren't responding to our requests, so eventually I flew to Scotland to visit the University of Glasgow Library, where I was able to study the original plans of the RMS Lusitania instead. Designed by Harland & Wolff's rival shipbuilders John Brown & Company, the Lusitania is sometimes thought of as the Titanic's sister ship, as it was similar in both its size and fate: three years after the Titanic hit the iceberg, the Lusitania was hit by a German U-boat off the south coast of Ireland—and most of its twelve hundred passengers and crew drowned while waiting to be rescued.

The University of Glasgow's archive was a great help, allowing us to repurpose the drawings for our show for a small fee. When I arrived at the library, the archivists had the plans waiting for me in a dimly lit room and armed me with a pair of white gloves so I could spend the day studying the documents. Each plan was more beautiful than the next, and we scanned almost twenty pieces to dress the drawing office set. We airbrushed out the name RMS Lusitania, hand-lettered the words R.M.S. Titanic, and assumed that nobody would know any better. It wasn't until the camera was about to start rolling that we were radioed from the set: one of the stagehands had pointed out that the Titanic actually had three working funnels, and this ship seemed to have four. In the early 1900s funnels were symbols of speed and safety and the White Star Line wanted their newest ocean liner to be able to compete with its rival, at least on the outside: the Titanic's fourth smokestack was actually only a dummy, containing a first-class smoking room. The production designer decided to let this one go, though—the chances of the camera lingering on the drawing long enough for our error to be spotted were slim.

SKETCHES FOR SCIENCE FICTION ICONOGRAPHY

How do you research a time that hasn't happened yet? I once worked briefly on a science fiction movie about a spaceship set two hundred years in the future. The spacecraft needed all kinds of directional signage as well as interactive screens displaying information. My first instinct was to study the design on the full-color interactive screens we carry in our pockets now—Isn't this the future?—but the production designer steered me in the direction of simpler navigational signage instead, more like the symbolism you might see in an older film. The 1970s were a golden age for sci-fi, and audiences still buy that era's science-fiction design more readily than anything that resembles the styles of modern Apple products. We started to create a navigational language for the spacecraft with a graphic simplicity to it, almost like old road signage. But just as we got going, the funding for the film was pulled, and all the construction work underway stopped. Another production company bought the script and made the film in the States with an entirely new cast and crew.

AIRLOCK

ARTIFICIAL
GRAVITY AREA

ARTIFICIAL
GRAVITY ABSENT

AXE

BRIDGE

CARGO
STOWAGE

COMM
CENTRE

COMMAND
DECK

CUSTOMER
HELPLINE

DECK Nº

ELEVATORS

EMERGENCY
MANUALS

FACE
MASKS

FIRE
EXTINGUISHERS

FIREWALL

HAZARDOUS
AREA

INFOMAT

INTERSTELLAR
MESSAGING

OBSERVATORY

RUSSIAN
LESSONS

CHAPTER 3

<u>ZUBROWKA</u>

THE TOWN OF GÖRLITZ SITS SO CLOSE TO GERMANY'S EASTERNMOST
BORDER THAT DURING THE MAKING OF <u>THE GRAND BUDAPEST HOTEL</u>,
WE COULD LITERALLY WALK OVER A WOODEN FOOTBRIDGE AND HAVE
OUR LUNCH IN POLAND. WE HARDLY EVER DID, THOUGH: WE ONLY
HAD ONE WINTER TO TRANSFORM THE TOWN INTO WES ANDERSON'S
FICTITIOUS COUNTRY OF ZUBROWKA, AND TIME WAS AGAINST US.

At the start of The Grand Budapest Hotel's production, in late September 2012 in Studio Babelsberg in Berlin, it wasn't entirely clear which crew members would go with Wes Anderson to Görlitz and which would stay behind. I assumed I'd be staying, and only the shooting crew and some department heads would go to the location. I'd probably be of more use in the city, I thought, where I was near the suppliers. Besides, the graphic designers don't generally need to be near the set. But by the end of that first month in Berlin, we received a memo from the production office announcing that the entire crew would be packing up and heading east for the duration of the project: every single last one of us, along with the cast, to live in the town and make it our home for the winter.

Görlitz didn't suffer any bomb damage during World War II, and most of its beautiful old art deco architecture still stands. The film's production designer, Adam Stockhausen, was to turn the town's great but dilapidated department store into the Grand Budapest's interiors, and our offices would be based inside the building, too. It was a peculiar place to work: the art department set up on the upper floor, and the film shot on the lower floors, with the architecture's mezzanine structure allowing us to look down at the action below. To be upstairs making fake fingerprint samples, listening to the gunshots of staged police chases underneath us, felt weirdly palpable— but at the same time completely surreal.

Zubrowka's imaginary status meant we couldn't rely on creating facsimiles of state-issued documents like we could for stories set in real countries. Flags, passports, coats of arms, postage stamps, and banknotes are all pieces that we would usually source, clean up, and reproduce. But in this case, the script identified the Klubeck as the official Zubrowkan currency, and we would have to design it entirely from scratch.

The volume of original material required by a story like this is enormous, and as soon as I read the script, I knew I wouldn't be able to produce all the graphic pieces alone. On top of the graphic props outlined in the screenplay, the set decorator, Anna Pinnock, also had her own list of graphics that she'd need for background dressing—piles of office documents, hotel ledgers, stencils for crates—all the things that wouldn't necessarily be mentioned in a script but that a shoot can't do without. Between our lists there were almost four hundred different pieces that would need to be designed and manufactured in the following weeks. It was clear that we'd also need to recruit a supporting graphic designer, and we were lucky to find Liliana Lambriev, who had worked on all types of period movies set in both Germany and in fictitious worlds. On our first day together in Görlitz, we, along with two assistants, Molly and Miguel, set up our little graphics studio at the top of five flights of stairs and got to work.

Designing for Wes Anderson was exhilarating. I hadn't worked for an auteur before, and it was both an honor and a challenge to help turn his ideas into tactile objects. While every prop started out with a reference from history, each had to be developed to suit the camera, the story, and his visual style. He experimented with every piece we made for him, and we would amend each design until it was just the right balance of historical Eastern Europe and the amplified, make-believe Zubrowka. We spent more time developing each piece than we might have done on other films, but we also had more prep time—I began working on the project three months before shooting was scheduled to start, which seemed like a real luxury compared to the six weeks I was used to.

After a while, living in this remote town for the winter began to feel like life imitating art—we were all part of a large, rambling Andersonian family in a half-imaginary, half-tangible world. The crew stayed in a hotel overlooking the border river—we were living in Germany but looking out at Poland from our bedroom windows—and in the early mornings, we could walk to work on a path through a tall forest to the town center. By mid-November the first snow had fallen; by the beginning of December the first Christmas market had opened. It was strange to be out shopping for groceries on a Saturday morning (cold meats and cheese that could be prepared in a kitchenless hotel room) and be standing in a line at the checkout behind Ralph Fiennes or Bill Murray. The more props we made, the more buildings the art department transformed, the more the line between fact

and fiction blurred. The camera wasn't scheduled to start rolling
until January, but we were so knee-deep in preparation in the
weeks leading up to Christmas that as soon as the holiday hit,
I flew home to Ireland and slept for the better part of a week,
knowing that we'd be in the thick of it until we wrapped, at the
end of March.

LETTERING SKETCHES FOR HOTEL SIGNAGE

In modern commercial design, it's common practice to keep any given business identity consistent. Shop logos look exactly the same on their storefronts as they do on their web-sites as they do on their paper bags—it's the matching luggage of graphic design. It wasn't always this way, though. In the early 1900s, the style of an establishment's lettering was dictated by the material: the name on the iron gates was designed by a blacksmith, while the font on the stationery was chosen by the printer. It's unlikely that these two craftsmen would ever have laid eyes on each other, let alone swapped style notes.

When we draw logotypes for use in period film-making, we can't just copy and paste lettering from one digital drawing to the next and hope that it will feel authentic. In The Grand Budapest Hotel, Wes Anderson asked us to draw up multi-ple versions of the hotel's logotype, the style of each dependent on how and when it would have been made. The printed letterhead on the hotel's 1930s stationery shows a hand-drawn double-lined style, while the name above the main entrance has a rounded, more flourished lettering, as if it were shaped from brass. The bulb-lit letters spelling "HOTEL" are different shapes yet again, designed to fit the arches of the window frames. Later, in the 1960s, simple sans-serif capitals are lined up on a rail on the communist-era roof, with plastic green and yellow light boxes showing the name above the awning.

The most familiar of all the Grand Budapest lettering is probably the hotel's name on the original 1930s rooftop: the letters are angular, with jagged serifs that look as if they were designed on the spot by whoever was operating the circular saw. The space between the "A" and the "N" in "GRAND" seems a little on the wide side, but this irregular kerning was intentional, almost as if, at some point in the building's lifetime, a letter had come loose from the roof and a hotel caretaker had climbed up a ladder to stick it back up again.

GRAND BUDAPEST HOTEL

GRAND BUDAPEST

HOTEL

HOTEL

GRAND
BUDAPEST

THE MENDL'S BOX

The pink Mendl's boxes appeared, at some point, in almost every set in the 1930s chapters of <u>The Grand Budapest Hotel</u>. The prop master, Robin Miller, had hundreds of pieces fabricated, using a specialist box maker in Berlin, while Lili liaised with the screen-printer, who silk-screened the patisserie's emblem onto each one in bright red ink. The graphic was all rendered manually: the word "MENDL'S" by our illustrator and the rest of the lettering and filigree by myself, which, because it never went through a digital spell check, meant that the extra "T" I'd inad-vertently included in the word "pâtisserie" went unnoticed until about halfway through the shoot. I was embarrassed to have made

such a glaring error on a hero prop, especially because at that point we'd already shot on hundreds of boxes. But the producers were pragmatic about it: the mistake would be fixed in post-production, at least on any boxes that were legible to the audience.

Months later, after the movie's release, imita-tion Mendl's boxes began to appear for sale on eBay. Some of these weren't too far off from the original—although the particular shades of red and pink and the very specific texture of the ribbon were hard to match exactly. It could always be confirmed, though, if a box had really made an appearance in the movie—it had that extra "T" in "pâtisserie."

THREE KLUBECK BANKNOTES

Zubrowka's official emblem—an eagle attacking a dove—can be seen all over the state's printed ephemera as well as on its official currency, the Klubeck. The banknotes were printed in three denominations: 10, 20, and 100, each differentiated by size and color. The 100 Klubeck notes seem quite big compared to modern money, but they were based on historical examples—Wes directed us toward the dimensions of the very large French francs from the turn of the last century.

ZUBROWKAN POSTAGE STAMPS → →

Ludwig's prison escape map was described as being a crude but highly detailed map and floor plan of the castle compound, which Gustave admires as showing great artistic promise. Reading a scripted description of a main character pausing over a graphic piece like this is a sure sign that it might get a close-up on the cinema screen: movie characters rarely talk about the graphics.

The exterior of the prison was shot at Kriebstein Castle in Saxony and the interiors at Zittau, an abandoned prison. (It's not uncommon for filmmakers to use two different locations to depict the inside and outside of a building.) We were able to piece together Ludwig's floor plan by studying the location team's photographs of the two places and by following his character's scripted dialogue, which describes both the structure of the prison and all its comic elements in some detail—the barbed wire on the containment walls; the broad-gauge iron bars on every door, vent, and window; the seventy-two guards on the floor and sixteen more in the towers; and the 325-foot drop into a moat full of crocodiles.

The reverse of the map also needed designing, as it was meant to look as if it had been drawn on a piece of packaging paper. If we were to make packaging paper we would need a packaging label. A packaging label would need franking marks. Franking marks would need postage stamps—and postage stamps for a fictitious empire would need a fictitious emperor, too. What does the emperor of Zubrowka look like? Even though he's never mentioned in the script, he still had to exist somehow. The woodcut image on the stamp was drawn by our illustrator, Jan, and inspired by an old picture of the German President Hindenburg, with an enormous (and historically accurate) mustache.

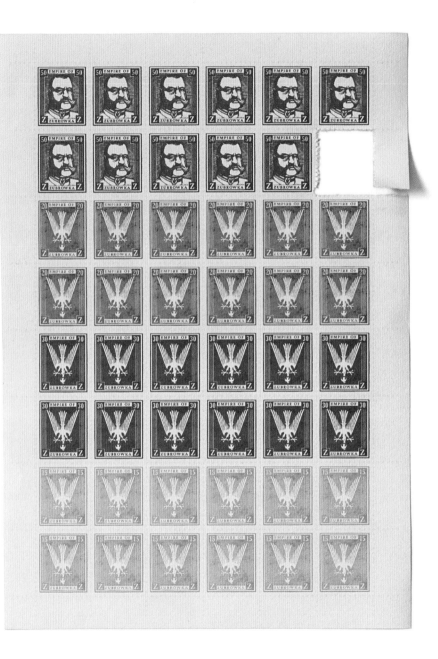

LUDWIG'S PRISON ESCAPE MAP (FOLDED)

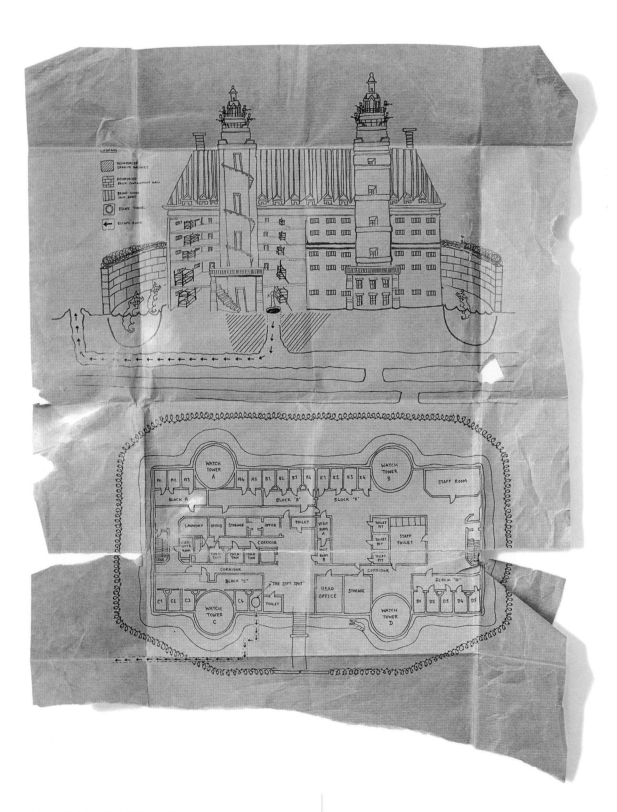

LUDWIG'S PRISON ESCAPE MAP (UNFOLDED)

SKETCHES FOR KEY FOB DESIGNS

LUGGAGE TAGS

Five other grand hotels exist within the <u>Grand Budapest</u>'s story: the Ritz Imperial, Chateau Luxe, Hotel Côte du Cap, Palazzo Principessa, and the Excelsior Palace. Initially seen in the background as travel stickers dotted across Madame D.'s luggage, each hotel gets a close-up of its own when Gustave calls on the concierges of the Society of the Crossed Keys to help him after he escapes from prison.

1960s RESTAURANT MENU → →

As Mr. Moustafa orders dinner from a menu in the dining room, the painting <u>Boy with Apple</u> is visible on its cover. Scripted to have been painted by "Johannes Van Hoytl the Younger," Wes had commissioned the English figurative artist Michael Taylor to paint the original oil. But instead of printing a photographic reproduction of <u>Boy with Apple</u> on the menu, we were directed to think of this piece as a second painting—a watercolor, perhaps—as if it had been created in tribute to the original by one of the hotel's elderly guests. In cases like this, it can be more effective to recruit someone to create a piece, rather than try to imitate a certain style in the art department. In the spirit of authenticity, and with only a couple of days to turn the artwork around, I called on someone who fit the bill that I could also depend on to deliver: my seventy-year-old mother, Mary, back home in Snowdonia in North Wales.

Boy with Apple   *Zubrowka*

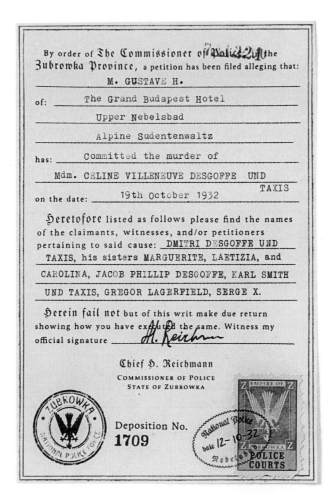

By order of The Commissioner of Police in the Zubrowka Province, a petition has been filed alleging that:

M. GUSTAVE H.

of: The Grand Budapest Hotel

Upper Nebelsbad

Alpine Sudentenwaltz

has: Committed the murder of

Mdm. CELINE VILLENEUVE DESGOFFE UND TAXIS

on the date: 19th October 1932

Heretofore listed as follows please find the names of the claimants, witnesses, and/or petitioners pertaining to said cause: DMITRI DESGOFFE UND TAXIS, his sisters MARGUERITE, LAETIZIA, and CAROLINA, JACOB PHILLIP DESGOFFE, KARL SMITH UND TAXIS, GREGOR LAGERFIELD, SERGE X.

Herein fail not but of this writ make due return showing how you have executed the same. Witness my official signature _____

Chief H. Reichmann
COMMISSIONER OF POLICE
STATE OF ZUBROWKA

Deposition No.
1709

EMPIRE OF
POLICE
COURTS

GUSTAVE'S DEPOSITION

At the beginning of the production, when we were still in Berlin, the props team rented an original 1930s typewriter that we used to type some sample sheets. The typewriter was a huge, heavy cast-iron machine—an original German Adler—in perfect working order, and the noise it made when we banged on the keys disturbed the whole art department. We were supposed to return it after a week, but it ended up traveling all the way to Görlitz with us, as we found ourselves needing to use it for nearly all of Zubrowka's official documents— we just couldn't get a digital typewriter font to look as authentic as the real thing.

This is the last Will and Testament that I, Madame
Celine Villeneuve Desgoffe und Taxis

a resident and citizen of Lutz, Zubrowka, being of sound mind and disposing memory, do hereby make, publish and declare this document to be my last will and testament hereby revoking any and all wills and codicils by me at any time heretofore made.

I. I anticipate that included as a part of my property and estate at the time of my death will be tangible personal property of various kinds, characters and realms, including jewels and other items accumulated by me during my life.

II. I hereby specifically command my son, Dmitri Desgoffe und Taxis, Desgoffe und Taxis, herein appointed, shall have complete freedom and discretion as to disposal of any and all such property so long as he shall act in good faith and in the best interest of my estate and my beneficiaries, and his discretion so exercised shall not be subject to question by anyone whomsoever with special allowances for his sisters Marguerite, Laetizia, and Carolina.

III. I hereby expressly authorise my Executor and my Trustee, respectively and successively, to permit any beneficiary of any, and all trusts created hereunder to enjoy in specie the use or benefit of any jewellery, chattels, or other tangible personal property (exclusive of choses in action cash, stocks, bonds or other securities) which either my Executor or my Trustees may receive in kind and any Executor and my Trustees shall not be liable for any consumption, damage, injury to or loss of any tangible property so used, nor shall the beneficiaries of any trusts hereunder as their executor or administrators be liable for any consumption, damage, injury to or loss of any tangible personal property so used.

IV. If I am the owner of any property at the time of my death I instruct and empower only Executor and my Trustee (as the case may be) to hold such real estate for investment as to sell some or any portion thereof as my Executor or only Trustee (as the case may be) shall in his sole judgement determine to be for the best interest of my estate and the beneficiaries thereof.

V. After payment of all debts, expenses and taxes as directed under Item I hereof I give devise and bequeath all the rest residue and remainder of any estate including all lapsed legacies and devises and any property over which I have a power of appointment.

VI. If my estate is the beneficiary of any life insurance on any life at the time of my death, I direct that the proceeds then from will be used by my Executor in payment of the debts, expenses and taxes listed in Item I of this will, to the extent deemed admirable by the Executor. All such proceeds not so used are to be used by my Executor for the proper of satisfying the devises and bequests contained in Item IV herein.

Mdm. C.V.D.u.T.

VII. If my estate ... 2 of any life insurance on any listed in Item I of this will,

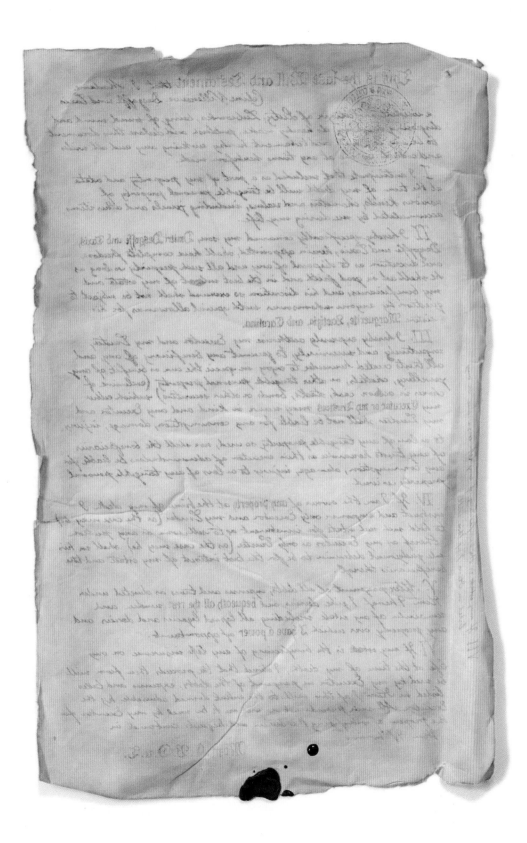

GRAND BUDAPEST

HOTEL

UPPER NEBELSBAD, ALPINE SUDETENWALTZ
ZUBROWKA
TELEGRAM ADDRESS:
GRANDBUDAPEST (NEBELSBAD)
TELEPHONE:
NEBELSBAD 43

For my dearest Gustave

With love,

Madame D.

THE LAST WILL AND TESTAMENT OF MADAME D.
& MADAME D.'S NOTE TO GUSTAVE ← ←

According to the script, Madame D.'s last
will and testament had been drawn up before
the event of her husband's death, placing
its creation around 1886. We used a soft,
handmade Japanese paper that would take aging
well—torn edging and tea staining—and we
wrote the scrawled calligraphy with a dipping
pen and sepia ink to help make it look forty-
six years old. The kiss at the bottom of her
parting note to Gustave matched the pink
of her character's lip color exactly, which
we borrowed from Tilda Swinton's make-up
artist especially for the prop.

BOOK OF ROMANTIC POETRY, VOL. I → →

Zero's inscription to Agatha in the book of
romantic poetry is never seen in close-up on
the page but was, instead, used as subtitles
on the screen. Our first pass at this handwriting
was too formal—it looked like it had been carefully crafted by a calligrapher. (It had!) Wes
suggested that we show the actor Tony Revolori
how to use the dipping pen and ink and let him
copy the piece from the calligrapher, without
using a ruler or lined paper so that it had a
more natural feel to it. The resulting lettering
style genuinely looked like it had been written
by his character, and we traced it back into
the book, taking care to keep all its swirls
and curls intact.

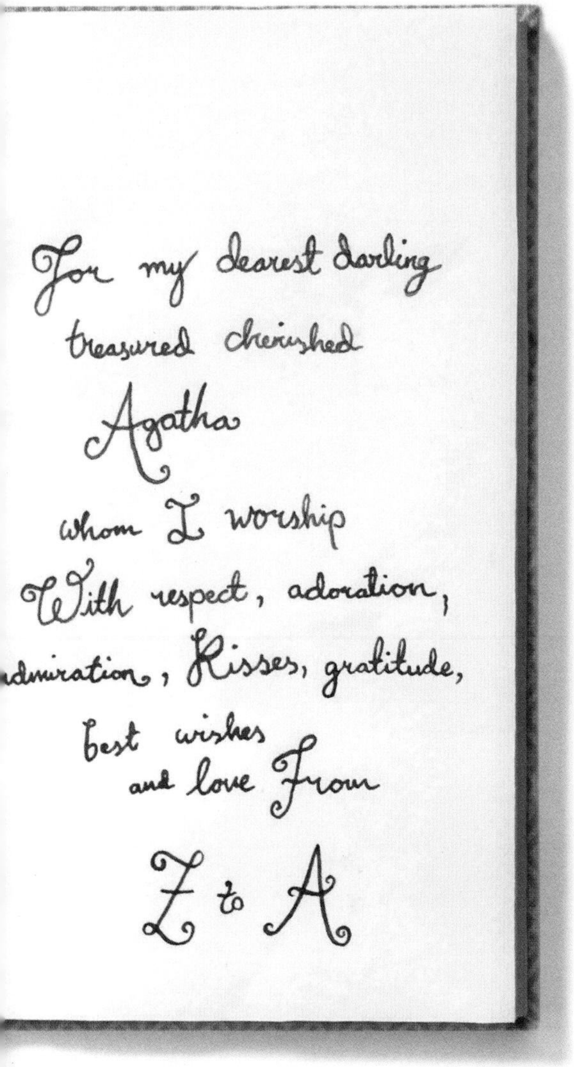

For my dearest darling
treasured cherished
Agatha
whom I worship
With respect, adoration,
admiration, Kisses, gratitude,
best wishes
and love From

Z to A

J. G. Jopling, Esq.
PRIVATE INQUIRY AGENT

JOPLING'S CALLING CARD

Jopling's calling card was letterpress-printed simply in black ink, with the text modestly center-aligned at a small point size. Based on layouts of real German cards from the 1930s, these pieces never detailed any contact information. Also known as "visiting cards," they were used as props within the social ritual of visiting the homes of friends and acquaintances—if you moved in upper-class circles, that is. The card would be presented to the servant upon opening the door, who would then carry it on a silver tray to the person you were calling for. If they were home, they might come down to see you. If they were home but not taking visitors, they would send their own card back down on the tray. If they were home, not taking visitors, and had no desire for you ever to call on them again, they would send their own card back in an envelope— a coded but widely understood dismissal.

½ kl-. Friday, October 19th, 1932 nr. 314

Trans-Alpine Yodel

Morning Edition

Weather East and northeast 10 to 20 m/s, strongest by the southeast coast. Some snowshowers in the southeast and east. Frost 0 to 12 degrees C, coldest inland in the north. Northeast 8 to 18 m/s, strongest wind in the southeast. Snowshowers in the north and east, but fair weather in the southwest. Frost widely 0 to 5 deg. Still northeast wind. Snowshowers in the north and east, but snow in the east in the evening. Fair weather in the southwest. Similar temperature. Northeasterly wind and widely some snow or snowshowers, especially in the north, but rain or drizzle by the east coast. Temperature widely 0 to 5 deg.

Announcements for interests of all kinds are written by the administrators of the Zubrowkian common general Trans Alpine Yodel newspaper, including politics, business, farming, bathing, and winter sports. Column millimeters in the advertising sections = 45mm wide, news sections 90mm wide, sports sections 90mm wide. Paper printed on 10a newsprint from Lyulped in Zubrowka. Inserts for singleweights of 20a to 30a to 40a (maximum). For special editions and special topics, readers may submit their enquiries to our archivist at the State Library in Lutz. Apply in writing.

All the news from across the nation
in two daily editions

RGN 2436 Zubrowka DL 254

WILL THERE BE WAR?

Tanks at Border

The highest ranking official uner the auspices of the Chancellor Principal Fridan resigned from his post under protest due to the mishandling of the Parradine Case. "I can no longer permit myself to be associated..." he murmured to the assembled tribunal before sort of trailing off. Later that afternoon, he was sighted in Krakauer Park sitting on a bench next to a blind old man. A reporter approached him tentatively and found him agreeable to a few words.

Q: What are your plans?

A: My retirement begins today. Frankly, it will be a great relief to me to unburden myself of the pressures of political life and the military establishment. I intend to travel without portfolio. Who knows where my wanderings may lead me.

Q: What of your family? Do they support your decision?

A: I did not inquire of them their opinions. They don't know one damn thing about it. Best

Talk of war remains general all along the border-counties and deep across the West Zubrowkian frontier. Those in doubt about the gravity of the situation woke up to sobering news this morning. The Barracuda Brigades of General von Schilling's iron tank division moved briskly into position above the good King's hunting grounds and trained their turret-sights on Lutz.

Silence from both the emperor and the parliamentary administration increased anxiety amongst the populace. Only the unpredictable mayor of Lutz, Mr. Barishnokov, spoke out in his own puzzling manner: "There will be no war. The men in charge know full well any escalation at this point can only mean mutual destruction, and believe you me, nobody wants everybody to lose. In other words, they want somebody, at least, to win -- namely themselves. It just doesn't add up.

sibility of long-term peace.

War technology continues to evolve at a brisk pace, while philosophy and theology remain at a general stand-still. Hope is fading, replaced by the blunt ideologies of today's vanguard and their firm, misguided beliefs.

Why do we fight? This question has been on people's lips consistently all through the season. Some cling to their belief in a "noble savage" but more and more the cognoscenti have been forced to admit it: it does not look good. The development of a highly enlightened intellectual mittel-Europa limned with the glow of artistic abundance, soaring with the greatest music, architecture, literature, poetry, and scientific advance in the history of human-kind -- has lead us directly down the path of self-destruction and blackest evil. There can be no satisfactory expla-

Order from Rathaus: Stop Traffic

Challenging weather Conditions during the past weeks have lead to the necessity of the strict enforcement of a long-standing ban on horse-cart travel in the back-streets of Upper Lutz.

On the law books for the past fifty-odd years, the regulation was nevertheless little-known and rarely called upon. However, in part due to aging cobblestones, and especially due to slick black-ice left over from the early frost, the new policy seen in full effect last week brought dozens of unwitting violators down to the Rathaus where they paid fines and argued for clemency. "Be warned," was the message from the Burger Meister. Challenging weather Conditions during the past weeks have lead to the necessity of the strict enforcement of a long-standing ban on horse-cart travel in the back-streets of Upper Lutz.

Avalanche in Brauenesshotten

An avalanche in the north-western region of Zubrow-

TRANS-ALPINE YODEL

When Zero buys the hotel's daily stack of newspapers from the press kiosk, the shot is framed by two bold posters, each based on the brightly colored, block-printed boards that declared the latest headlines in the 1900s. The Trans-Alpine Yodel was Zubrowka's paper of record: all the news from across the nation, in two daily editions.

ZUBROWKA'S PAPER OF RECORD

Trans-Alpine Morning Edition Yodel

TWO DAILY EDITIONS

Trans-Alpine
MORNING EDITION **Yodel**

POLICE REPORT

The police report showing Deputy Kovacs's six
remaining fingerprints began its life as a real
police document from the 1930s, but as its style
developed, it slowly turned into something more
comic, in line with the events of the script.
(Kovacs had lost four of his fingers in a slammed
door.) The fingerprints might look oversized,
but they were actually printed to scale—the
scale being Jeff Goldblum's hands.

This report is the property of the Zubrowkian National Police Force. Any attempt to copy, deface, or interfere with this document in any way shall result in immediate arrest.

Police Report

№ 36652 A
Date 23 OCTOBER
AH

MURDER

1. Victim DEPUTY KOVACS	2. Nature of Incident MURDER	3. Place of Incident KUNSTMUSEUM LUTZ
5. Time 7.15	UNKNOWN	6. Other notes NONE

Severe contusions to head and chest.
Excessive loss of blood. Severing of
all fingers on right hand. Fingers themselves not yet located and believed to be
have been deliberately removed (possibly by
killer). Very little indication of struggle.
Wrongful death. Body discovered in Egyptian
wing deep storage vault. Kunstmuseum
archives. Immediately transferred to Lutz
morgue for full autopsy.

LEFT HAND

RIGHT HAND

THE GRAND BUDAPEST HOTEL BOOK

The Grand Budapest Hotel's eponymous pink book
is my very favorite of all the props that I've
worked on—partly because it's so rare to get
to make artwork with the name of the movie
on it but also because it's the piece that both
opens and closes the film. In the beginning,
the girl in the beret brings the book to Lutz
Cemetery to pay tribute to its author, and at
the very end of the story, she sits on a bench
finishing the final chapter. Both of these scenes
were shot on the same day, on an overcast
Saturday at the end of March, our very last day
in Görlitz. We were supposed to be packing up
our graphics room—putting away our tools and
sorting everything into boxes—but the task
was abandoned in favor of all going down to
the set together, to watch the very last takes
of the movie and to hear Wes call wrap.

CHAPTER 4

<u>CONTINUITY</u>

CONTINUITY IS A MAJOR PART OF THE FILMMAKING PROCESS—
AND PROBABLY ALSO ONE OF THE MOST TEDIOUS, AS METICULOUS
NOTES NEED TO BE KEPT ON EVERY MINUTE DETAIL OF A SHOOT.
IT'S ONLY TEDIOUS UNTIL SOMETHING GOES WRONG, THOUGH;
THEN ALL OF A SUDDEN CONTINUITY ERRORS CAN SEEM LIKE THE
MOST FASCINATING PART OF A MOVIE.

When I was in film school, we were shown a movie clip of a man and a woman sitting outside a tent in the desert at night together, talking. I can't remember what their conversation was about, and I can't remember the name of the film. Out of context, the scene was largely unremarkable. But when we were asked to watch it again, this time concentrating on the props instead of the dialogue, we saw that in some shots the man was eating an apple, and after cutting back from the reverse shots of the woman, the apple had turned into a pear. The fruit changed from apple to pear and from pear to apple maybe five times during the course of the conversation, neither character distracted in any way by what was happening in front of them. Once we'd seen the mistake, it was impossible to unsee it: what had been relatively pedestrian dialogue now just seemed absurd. I remember feeling completely perplexed by this. How could something as obvious as this slip through the net? How did the director not notice? Or the art department? Or the script supervisor? How was it possible for an actor to pick up a pear one minute and an apple the next and not even realize that he was eating the wrong prop?

Now, after years spent making my own continuity errors, I get it. There are countless possible reasons for this mistake, but one of the most logical explanations concerns reshoots. I can imagine the director watching the scene months after the shoot in the editing suite, unhappy with a line of dialogue, and eventually deciding (not lightly) to take the crew back to the desert to shoot the conversation again. It is a year later at this point, and the continuity notes simply list the actor as eating fruit. The actor in question has eaten over a hundred pieces of fruit since he played this role and not even he remembers that the pear was really an apple. Back in the editing suite, the director is now happy with some lines of dialogue but wants to keep half of the original shots as they were. He understands there's a pear-shaped goof on the horizon, but the priority is the acting, not the objects that the actors are handling—confirmed years later, when the clip is played to a class of twenty film students, and nobody notices a thing.

Continuity, this "maintenance of continuous detail," is a major part of the filmmaking process—and probably also one of the most tedious. Overseen by the script supervisor, careful notes are taken about the set and all of its props as well as the actions of the characters. Did the actor take a drag on her cigarette before or after her first line of dialogue? When does she blow the smoke back out? Is the box in shot? What brand is she smoking? What height had the candle burnt to by the time she stubbed out the cigarette? These details are only tedious until something goes wrong. As soon as the audience is jolted out of their cinematic spell, continuity can suddenly become one of the most captivating things about an entire film.

In the art department, we have a responsibility to continuity before our props even land on set, starting when we read the script. Sitting down with a hard copy of the screenplay is the first thing a graphic designer does on any job, almost as soon as we arrive at the studio. Reading through it with a highlighter, we mark any props, set pieces, or dressing that might be the responsibility of the graphics team. Sometimes these things are entirely obvious: a map, or a menu, for example; other times, less so. If we read that one character pulls out a handkerchief and dries another character's eyes, we have to ask whether that handkerchief will need a bespoke pattern, and if so, will that most likely come from graphics or costume? The gray areas that sometimes exist between the different departments are always highlighted and marked as a question. It's better to have every possibility listed than to face the wrath of a set decorator looking for a piece that you have no recollection of reading about whatsoever.

Any names or phrases that might be useful for set graphics also need to be highlighted in the script, even though they can often be hidden in lines of dialogue. In <u>The Boxtrolls</u>, for example, Eggs asks Winnie where he might find the Redhat Extermination Company. She tells him they operate down on Curd's Way, pointing at the street sign above their heads, and joking, "Milk turns into it!" It's the kind of conversation that might be easy for graphics to miss—a prop master I worked with once shook his head sadly and said, "Nobody in the art department ever reads the dialogue." It's true that a script can read less like a story and more like a steady stream of directions—we get used to reading in a way that highlights only the pieces we have a vested interest in.

Just the word "office" in a scene heading, for example, will always stop me in my tracks: I'm well-versed, at this stage, in keeping an eye out for any suggestion of bulletin boards and bookshelves and countless documents piled on desks. A sex scene, on the other hand, can usually be skimmed. In a sex scene, nobody ever pulls out a newspaper or starts looking at a map.

THE ROYAL THEATRE, LITTLE GRESHAM ST.
Mr. W. BROWN's
"THE ROSE OF ARDRAHAN"
Wednesday, May 25, 1891.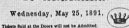
Tickets Sold at the Doors will not be Admitted.

THE ROYAL THEATRE, LITTLE GRESHAM ST.
Mr. W. BROWN's
"THE ROSE OF ARDRAHAN"
Wednesday, May 25, 1891.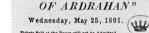
Tickets Sold at the Doors will not be Admitted.

THE ROYAL THEATRE, LITTLE GRESHAM ST.
Mr. W. BROWN's
"THE ROSE OF ARDRAHAN"
Wednesday, May 25, 1891.
Tickets Sold at t...

THE ROYAL
Mr.
"
OF
Wedne

THE ROYAL THEATRE, LITTLE WINDMILL ST.
Mr. W. BROWN's
"THE ROSE OF ARDRAHAN"
Wednesday, May 25, 1891.
Tickets Sold at the Doors will not be Admitted.

THE ROYAL THEATRE, LITTLE GRESHAM ST.
Mr. W. BROWN's
"THE ROSE OF ARDRAHAN"
Wednesday, May 25, 1891.
Tickets Sold at the Doors will not be Admitted.

THE ROYAL THEATRE, LITTLE GRESHAM ST.
Mr. W. BROWN's
"THE ROSE OF ARDRAHAN"
Wednesday, May 25, 1891.
Tickets Sold at the Doors will not be Admitted.

THE ROYAL
Mr.
"
Wedne

THE ROYAL THEATRE, LITTLE GRESHAM ST.
Mr. W. BROWN's
"THE ROSE OF ARDRAHAN"
Wednesday, May 25, 1891.
Tickets Sold at the Doors will not be Admitted.

THE ROYAL THEATRE, LITTLE GRESHAM ST.
Mr. W. BROWN's
"THE ROSE OF ARDRAHAN"
Wednesday, May 25, 1891.
Tickets Sold at the Doors will not be Admitted.

THE ROYAL THEATRE, LITTLE GRESHAM ST.
Mr. W. BROWN's
"THE ROSE OF ARDRAHAN"
Wednesday, May 25, 1891.
Tickets Sold at the Doors will not be Admitted.

THE ROYAL
Mr.
"
OF
Wedne

THE ROYAL THEATRE, LITTLE GRESHAM ST.
Mr. W. BROWN's
"THE ROSE OF ARDRAHAN"
Wednesday, May 25, 1891.
Tickets Sold at the Doors will not be Admitted.

THE ROYAL THEATRE, LITTLE GRESHAM ST.
Mr. W. BROWN's
"THE ROSE OF ARDRAHAN"
Wednesday, May 25, 1891.
Tickets Sold at the Doors will not be Admitted.

THE ROYAL THEATRE, LITTLE GRESHAM ST.
Mr. W. BROWN's
"THE ROSE OF ARDRAHAN"
Wednesday, May 25, 1891.
Tickets Sold at th...

THE ROYAL
Mr.
"T
OF
Wednes

THE ROYAL THEATRE, LITTLE GRESHAM ST.
Mr. W. BROWN's
"THE ROSE OF ARDRAHAN"
Wednesday, May 25, 1891.
Tickets Sold at the Doors will not be Admitted.

THE ROYAL THEATRE, LITTLE GRESHAM ST.
Mr. W. BROWN's
"THE ROSE OF ARDRAHAN"
Wednesday, May 25, 1891.
Tickets Sold at the Doors will not be Admitted.

THE ROYAL THEATRE, LITTLE GRESHAM ST.
Mr. W. BROWN's
"THE ROSE OF ARDRAHAN"
Wednesday, May 25, 1891.
Tickets Sold at the Doors will not be Admitted.

THE ROYAL
Mr
"
OF
Wednes
Tickets Sold at th...

THE ROYAL THEATRE, LITTLE GRESHAM ST.
Mr. W. BROWN's
"THE ROSE OF ARDRAHAN"
Wednesday, May 25, 1891.
Tickets Sold at the Doors will not be Admitted.

THE ROYAL THEATRE, LITTLE GRESHAM ST.
Mr. W. BROWN's
"THE ROSE OF ARDRAHAN"
Wednesday, May 25, 1891.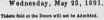
Tickets Sold at the Doors will not be Admitted.

THE ROYAL THEATRE, LITTLE GRESHAM ST.
Mr. W. BROWN's
"THE ROSE OF ARDRAHAN"
Wednesday, May 25, 1891.
Tickets Sold at the Doors will not be Admitted.

THE ROYAL
Mr.
"
OF
Wednes
Tickets at...

THE ROYAL THEATRE, LITTLE GRESHAM ST.
Mr. W. BROWN's
"THE ROSE OF ARDRAHAN"
Wednesday, May 25, 1891.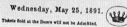
Tickets Sold at the Doors will not be Admitted.

THE ROYAL THEATRE, LITTLE GRESHAM ST.
Mr. W. BROWN's
"THE ROSE OF ARDRAHAN"
Wednesday, May 25, 1891.
Tickets Sold at the Doors will not be Admitted.

THE ROYAL THEATRE, LITTLE GRESHAM ST.
Mr. W. BROWN's
"THE ROSE OF ARDRAHAN"
Wednesday, May 25, 1891.
Tickets Sold at the Doors will not be Admitted.

THE ROYAL
M
"
OF
Wedne
Tickets Sold at t...

FORTY-NINE TICKETS

THE ROYAL THEATRE, LITTLE GRESHAM ST.
Mr. W. BROWN's
"THE ROSE OF ARDRAHAN"
Wednesday, May 25, 1891.
Tickets Sold at the Doors will not be Admitted.

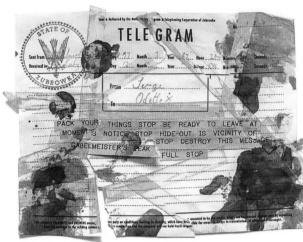

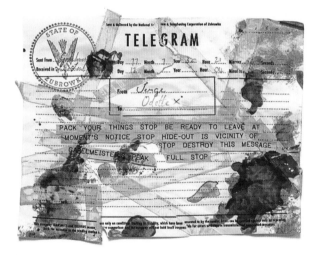

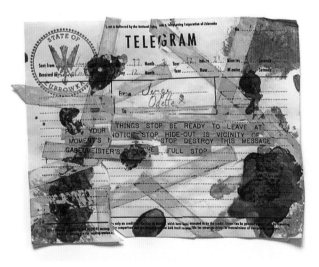

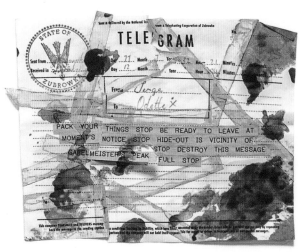

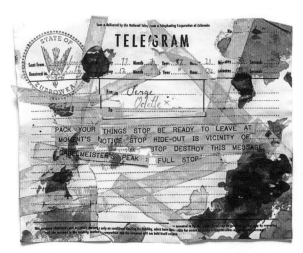

TWELVE YELLOW TELEGRAMS
(THE GRAND BUDAPEST HOTEL) ← ←

Because graphic props are, for the most part, made out of paper, they tend to be quite fragile. Film sets are dark, busy places, and while a candlestick can be wiped clean, if someone spills coffee on your telegram, it's all over. To avoid any issues with graphics while the shoot takes place, we make extra identical copies of any given paper prop, called "repeats."

Making identical repeats is laborious, so we use whatever tricks we can to speed up the process. If twelve maps need to be torn, then the easiest way to get all the tears in the exact same place is to stack the repeats on top of each other and rip them all at once. If a prop, like this yellow telegram, has really been through the mill, then we start a little production line to distress the object: one person oversees the ripping and another the stamping; one person sticks all the pieces back together again and another applies the blood.

MULTICOLOR SCRIPT PAGES FROM THE SHREDDER
AT THE END OF A SHOOT

It's industry standard for screenwriters to type a film script using twelve-point Courier New, with screenwriting software automatically formatting the leading, too. Being a fixed-width font, each letter in Courier takes up the same amount of horizontal space, whether that's an "I" or a "W." One page of a script roughly equals one minute of screen time. This means that screenwriters can then estimate that a one-hundred-and-twenty-page script will equate to a two-hour feature. It's true that some descriptions are lengthier than the shots themselves, and vice versa, but somehow, magically, it all evens out in the end.

It's a rookie mistake to write any detailed notes on the script itself. As a show progresses, changes are made by the screenwriters, and new pages are issued with precise instructions from the production office: "Replace white script pages 5–10 with new blue pages 5–7. All discarded pages to be shredded." Each batch of revisions is issued on a different-color paper, in a regimented order: first white (unrevised), then blue, yellow, pink, green, goldenrod (I love this unnecessarily romantic name for what is really just cheap orange copy paper), buff, salmon, cherry, and back to blue. The names of the paper colors are typed on the pages themselves, too, in case they get photocopied onto white at any point and turmoil ensues.

It might seem overly militant, but there's a reason why the phrase "all working to the same script" was coined. The chaos level of a film shoot can be judged by any crew member's dog-eared screenplay on wrap: if it's still mostly white, it was probably relatively straightforward, but less so if the stack of pages are now a paper rainbow.

Instead of writing notes on a page that will most likely have to be shredded, we write all our lists in what we call "script breakdowns"— essentially, spreadsheets containing detailed notes about any items relevant to our own department. In graphics, this can take at least a week to write properly, and we go over everything with a fine-tooth comb, including continuity minefields. If we've highlighted a line in the script describing a character being asked to show their identification, for example, we can't assume that the passport he presents won't be seen earlier in the shoot, too. Perhaps he'll also need it during a later scene, when he's simply packing up his suitcase, before traveling? To make things even more complicated, it may be that these particular scenes aren't going to be shot in story order, and the prop master will need the final passport earlier than the script suggests. We won't know the order of things until a preliminary shooting schedule is issued by the assistant directors—and even then it's liable to change substantially.

9 April 1521.

9 April 1521.

9 April 1521.

9 April 1521.

9 April 1521.

9 April 1521.

9 April 1521.

9 April 1521.

9 April 1521.

9 April 1521.

9 April 1521.

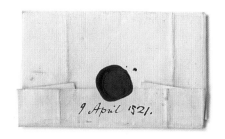

9 April 1521.

9 April 1521.

9 April 1521.

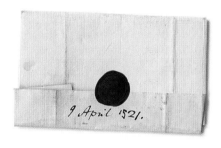

9 April 1521.

9 April 1521.

9 April 1521.

9 April 1521.

9 April 1521.

9 April 1521.

Script breakdowns and nervous breakdowns go hand in hand. Every spreadsheet I compile, I start out excited at the prospect of all the new, interesting pieces I'll have to create and end up wondering how I'm going to achieve any of it in the given time frame. Shooting a film in story order is almost unheard of, although there are some famous exceptions: E.T. was shot almost completely in chronological order, as Steven Spielberg wanted his young cast to be able to express the emotional arc of making and saying goodbye to a friend. The Shining was scheduled for a one-hundred-day shoot but ended up taking two hundred and fifty days—Stanley Kubrick shot chronologically so that he could add and make changes to the story as he went.

Usually, it isn't cost-effective or efficient to repeatedly move a film crew, setting up all their rigs and lights time and time again. Instead, the assistant directors schedule every shot in the entire movie prioritizing (a) location and (b) actor availability. All the hotel scenes, for example, will be shot in one go over several weeks no matter what kind of action is scripted. Then the entire crew will relocate to another set (a "unit move") and shoot all the prison scenes there. This lumping together of what can be quite varied scenes—

often chronologically far apart in a story—can be confusing, and personally I would not want to be a script supervisor or an assistant director for all the money in the world.

In turn, I'm pretty sure the one thing the assistant directors don't give a second thought about when they're scheduling a movie is graphic design: we are at the bottom of the food chain. I learned this the hard way on my first job, on the set of the third season of The Tudors (Showtime, 2009), when a last-minute schedule change meant that the antique maps I was having flatbed printed on vellum in England wouldn't arrive in Ireland by courier in time. The maps were crucial to the scene—Henry VIII was scripted to be poring over them, deciding how to invade France—but looking back, I'm not entirely sure what possessed me to take this issue to the First Assistant Director while he was coordinating a noisy medieval court scene on the set of "Westminster Palace." I explained the situation about the vellum, the courier, the flat-bed printing, and then waited for him to say he would change the schedule accordingly. He didn't, of course. I quietly printed the maps locally on heavy paper instead and made a mental note never to bother an A.D. about a prop again.

SKETCHES OF TWO US FLAGS

Filmmaking tricks—the repeats, multiple takes, reverse shots—can land us in trouble with continuity. Or, specifically, land us on the Internet Movie Database's goofs page, an online rabbit hole of our biggest failures, all meticulously documented by a film's audience. I love reading about these goofs. They morbidly fascinate me now that it's too late to change anything. Some are brilliantly pedantic (dates corresponding with the correct weekdays on a wall calendar); others seem kind of obvious in hindsight (cutting from a snowy winter to a leafy summer on the same story day). The guidelines for submissions to the IMDB website try to steer nitpickers toward identifying errors that are relevant or interesting—would this observation impress someone at a party?—and away from criticizing

a filmmaker's artistic license. (Yes, we all know there is no sound in space.)

Mostly, the mistakes registered are historical anachronisms: cars that didn't exist yet in 1960; violins played resting under chins in the 1400s (the actors should have held them to their stomachs). These kinds of corrections are educational; I can justify spending an hour scrolling through them in order to stop myself from making the same mistakes in the future. Not being American, for example, I hadn't stopped to think about the number of stars on the US flag in 1957, before Hawaii and Alaska were states, but I'll be sure to the next time I'm drawing one up for a period piece.

48 STAR FLAG 1912 - 1959

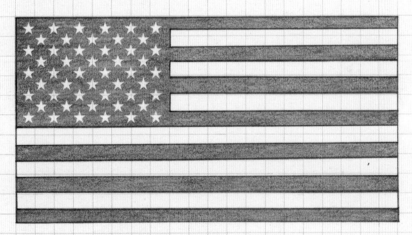

50 STAR FLAG 1960 - PRESENT

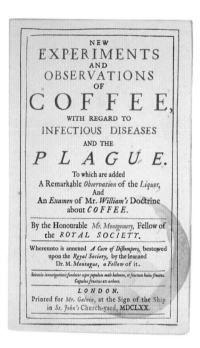

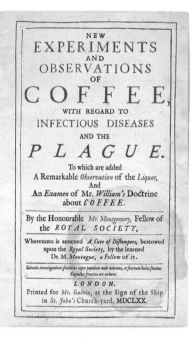

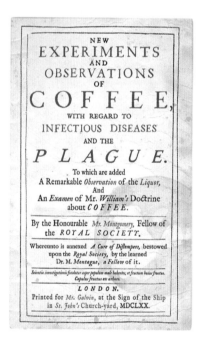

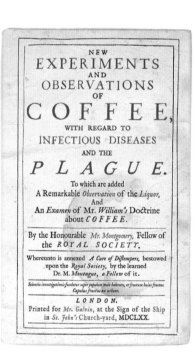

NEW
EXPERIMENTS
AND
OBSERVATIONS
OF
COFFEE,
WITH REGARD TO
INFECTIOUS DISEASES
AND THE
PLAGUE.

To which are added
A Remarkable *Observation* of the *Liquor*,
And
An *Examen* of Mr. *William's* Doctrine
about *COFFEE.*

By the Honourable *Mr. Montgomery*, Fellow of
the *ROYAL SOCIETY.*

Whereunto is annexed *A Cure of Distempers*, bestowed
upon the *Royal Society*, by the learned
Dr. M. *Montague*, a *Fellow* of it.

*Scientia investigationis fundatur super populum male habentes, et fructum huius fructus.
Capulus fructus ex arbore.*

LONDON.
Printed for *Mr. Galvin*, at the Sign of the Ship
in *St. John's* Church-yard, **MDCLXX.**

NEW
EXPERIMENTS
AND
OBSERVATIONS
OF
COFFEE,
WITH REGARD TO
INFECTIOUS DISEASES
AND THE
PLAGUE.

To which are added
A Remarkable *Observation* of the *Liquor*,
And
An *Examen* of Mr. *William's* Doctrine
about *COFFEE.*

By the Honourable *Mr. Montgomery*, Fellow of
the *ROYAL SOCIETY.*

Whereunto is annexed *A Cure of Distempers*, bestowed
upon the *Royal Society*, by the learned
Dr. M. *Montague*, a *Fellow* of it.

*Scientia investigationis fundatur super populum male habentes, et fructum huius fructus.
Capulus fructus ex arbore.*

LONDON.
Printed for *Mr. Galvin*, at the Sign of the Ship
in *St. John's* Church-yard, **MDCLXX.**

NEW
EXPERIMENTS
AND
OBSERVATIONS
OF
COFFEE,
WITH REGARD TO
INFECTIOUS DISEASES
AND THE
PLAGUE.

To which are added
A Remarkable *Observation* of the *Liquor*,
And
An *Examen* of Mr. *William's* Doctrine
about *COFFEE.*

By the Honourable *Mr. Montgomery*, Fellow of
the *ROYAL SOCIETY.*

Whereunto is annexed *A Cure of Distempers*, bestowed
upon the *Royal Society*, by the learned
Dr. M. *Montague*, a *Fellow* of it.

*Scientia investigationis fundatur super populum male habentes, et fructum huius fructus.
Capulus fructus ex arbore.*

LONDON.
Printed for *Mr. Galvin*, at the Sign of the Ship
in *St. John's* Church-yard, **MDCLXX.**

NEW
EXPERIMENTS
AND
OBSERVATIONS
OF
COFFEE,
WITH REGARD TO
INFECTIOUS DISEASES
AND THE
PLAGUE.

To which are added
A Remarkable *Observation* of the *Liquor*,
And
An *Examen* of Mr. *William's* Doctrine
about *COFFEE.*

By the Honourable *Mr. Montgomery*, Fellow of
the *ROYAL SOCIETY.*

Whereunto is annexed *A Cure of Distempers*, bestowed
upon the *Royal Society*, by the learned
Dr. M. *Montague*, a *Fellow* of it.

*Scientia investigationis fundatur super populum male habentes, et fructum huius fructus.
Capulus fructus ex arbore.*

LONDON.
Printed for *Mr. Galvin*, at the Sign of the Ship
in *St. John's* Church-yard, **MDCLXX.**

FOURTEEN ENVELOPES (VITA & VIRGINIA)

Handwriting for background pieces can be calligraphed and then scanned and reproduced with a printer to make multiple repeats, with touches of ink applied here and there to give the writing back some of its glint. For hero pieces, writing with ink directly onto the correct paper is preferable. If a prop is intended to be destroyed—e.g., the prop is ripped up by the actor or splattered with blood as part of the action—we could make up to twenty repeats, to cover as many takes as the director might need to capture the action. "Destroying" a prop doesn't have to involve blood or ripping—an actor scripted to be simply opening an envelope in shot could require repeats as well.

ROMA
·HOTEL·
HASSIER

Mrs Virginia Woolf
52 Tavistock Square
London W C 1
England

ROMA
·HOTEL·
HASSIER

Mrs Virginia Woolf
52 Tavistock Square
London W C 1
England

ROMA
·HOTEL·
HASSIER

Mrs Virginia Woolf
52 Tavistock Square
London W C 1
England

ROMA
·HOTEL·
HASSIER

Mrs Virginia Woolf
52 Tavistock Square
London W C 1
England

w   elite Publisher, and I shall get
                               regrets

HOTEL HASSIER·ROMA

DIRIMPETTO ALLA STAZIONE
COMPLETAMENTE RINNOVATO
ACQUA CORRENTE (FREDDA E) LUMINOSA
E TELEFONO INTERURBANO IN OGNI CAMERA
· DAMACA · RISTORANTE DI SERVIZIO
RINOMATO RISTORANTE
PREZZI MODICI

14 April

My darling Virginia,

        Will you come away with me next year?
I don't believe one ever knows people in their
own surroundings. One only knows them away;
divorced from all the little strings and
cobwebs of habit.

        Neither of us is the real, essential person
in these letters. Either I am at home and you
are strange, or you are at home and I am strange.
Here we should both be equally busy and equally
real. Will you come away with me?

        I hope that no one has ever yet, or
ever will, throw down a glove I was not ready
to pick up. You asked me to write a story for
you. On the peaks of mountains, and beside
green lakes, I am writing it for you. I shut
my eyes to the blue of gentians, to the coral
of androsace; I shut my ears to the bawling
of rivers, I shut my nose to the scent of
pines; I concentrate on my story. Perhaps you

TWELVE MIX TAPES

Twelve cassette tapes handwritten with
identical lettering, as an action graphic
to be destroyed on camera.

CHAPTER 5

<u>LANGUAGE</u>

THE LANGUAGE WE USE IN A FILM'S BACKGROUND GRAPHICS CAN
ADD TO THE DRAMA: OLD-FASHIONED ADVERTISING SLOGANS
CAN CREATE A CERTAIN ATMOSPHERE, INSTRUCTIONAL SIGNAGE
CAN HELP MOVE A STORY FORWARD, AND EVEN THE TINIEST
GRAMMATICAL DETAILS CAN CONJURE UP AN ENTIRELY DIFFERENT
PLACE AND TIME.

Books of historic street photography make great resources for re-creating city signage. In Philip Davies's <u>Panoramas of Lost London</u> (2011), a photograph of a hand-painted signboard, nailed high up on a café's exterior wall, advertises STEWED EELS & MASHED POTATOES in blocky capitals. It's the line underneath that's the most telling, though, with its flourished lettering spelling: "Always Ready." The eel was the fast food of the time—the hot dog of the 1800s.

During the making of <u>Penny Dreadful</u>, when we transformed modern Dublin into Victorian London, Davies's book became our art department manual—all of its beautiful black-and-white photography plastered with bright sticky notes marking the best visual references. Without a reference, it can be impossible to think up marketing copy that feels authentic to its day. While "eel and mash" can probably be guessed at, the "always ready" part wouldn't necessarily come to mind.

We can paint a picture of a specific time just by lettering a few choice words onto the hanging shop signs that dress a street scene. "Painless tooth extraction," advertised outside a Victorian dentist's office, now sounds suspiciously like an exaggeration. Dentistry in the 1800s was anything but painless. The gouging out of rotting teeth was a common cure for toothache, and toothache was common: in 1874, a tax on sugar was repealed, making sweets readily available to the working classes for the first time. Replacement teeth, though, were less affordable: grave robbers sold real human canines and molars at extortionate rates, owing to the long, cold nights they spent pulling them from the jaws of corpses. Persistent thieving was evident in the clause on the pawnbroker's window warning that money would only be lent "on all goods honestly come by," goods ranging from wooden legs and spectacles to full sets of teeth.

Death comes to everyone in the end and was amicably marketed by one London undertaker with the tagline "Funerals to suit all classes"—a nice acknowledgment of a social divide that today's businesses prefer not to mention. The average life expectancy of a Victorian Londoner was about thirty-eight years, but children from poorer homes were lucky to make it past five. Scarlet fever, tuberculosis, cholera, and smallpox were all rife in the city, and the information published on their various preventions and cures sometimes seemed, well, questionable in hindsight.

Cholera, one of the world's deadliest diseases, is an intestinal infection spread through contaminated water. In 1800s England, though, people believed that it was passed on through "smells in the air," as well as a whole host of other supposed, and super- stitious, contamination processes. Cholera, then, was widely believed to be completely unavoidable. How could you dodge "bad air and fear" in London's slums? It was futile. Give up. Bad air and fear were everywhere.

STEWED EELS & MASHED POTATOES: ALWAYS READY
(PENNY DREADFUL)

Archival photograph of Nile Street, Woolwich
c. 1900, used as reference research for street
scenes in and around East London in 1891.

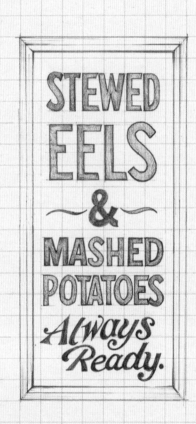

SKETCH FOR SIGNAGE (PENNY DREADFUL)

NOTICE.

PREVENTIVES OF

CHOLERA!

Published by order of the Sanitary Committee, under the sanction of the Medical Counsel.

DO NOT BREATHE BAD AIR

SLEEP and CLOTHE warm and do not sleep or sit in a draught of air. Avoid getting wet. Attend immediately to *All Disorders of the Bowels*.

ABSTAIN FROM FEAR!

☞ *PRESERVE A CALM COMPOSURE OF MIND*

The Depressing Passion of Fear, when cultivated

EXCITES THE DISEASE.

Medicine and Medical Advice can be had by THE POOR, at all hours of the day and night, by applying at the Station House.

CALEB S. WOODHULL. *Mayor*

JAMES KELLY, *Chairman of Sanitary Committee.*

STREET POSTER: CHOLERA! (PENNY DREADFUL)

Cholera was once one of London's biggest killers; the spread of misinformation about the disease was almost as potent as the spread of the disease itself. The wording on this street poster was paraphrased from "A Plain and Practical Treatise on the Epidemic Cholera Designed for Popular Instruction," a document published by a doctor in 1832 that only exacerbated the paranoia that you could catch the disease simply by being afraid of it. "Preserve a calm composure of mind," the doctor warned. "The depressing passion of fear, when cultivated, excites the disease." His advice is completely outdated and inaccurate, though: cholera is now known to be spread by contaminated food and water, not "bad air."

SKETCH FOR DENTIST'S SIGN (PENNY DREADFUL)

GEO. KING

FUNERALS
TO SUIT ALL
CLASSES.

EST. 1850

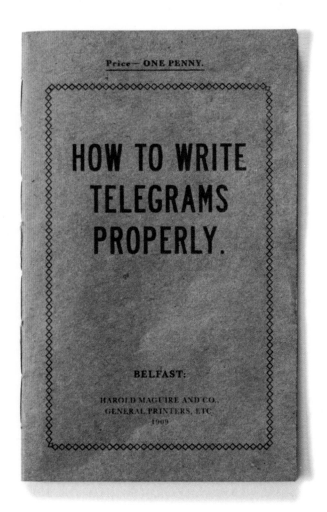

HOW TO WRITE TELEGRAMS PROPERLY
(TITANIC: BLOOD AND STEEL)

"As one would expect, wording telegrams requires a certain degree of care and consideration. A balance must be struck to convey a concise message without the extravagance of unnecessary words." Telegrams were the tweets of 1909: an exercise in keeping to the point. This pamphlet, though, includes tips on how not to come across as impolite in the process: "Let us protect the word 'please' and habitually include it in all our correspondences." Paraphrased from real telegraph-office-issued advice in early 1900s England, this was created for use as background dressing for a desk in Titanic: Blood and Steel. It's highly unlikely that the booklet was read by anyone other than the extra playing the office clerk—but since any shot can stretch out over hours of takes, we know that at least one person presumably gave it a good read.

R.M.S. "TITANIC".

APRIL 14, 1912.

LUNCHEON.

CONSOMMÉ FERMIER   COCKIE LEEKIE

FILLETS OF BRILL

EGG À L'ARGENTEUIL

CHICKEN À LA MARYLAND

CORNED BEEF, VEGETABLES, DUMPLINGS

FROM THE GRILL.

GRILLED MUTTON CHOPS

MASHED, FRIED & BAKED JACKET POTATOES

CUSTARD PUDDING

APPLE MERINGUE   PASTRY

BUFFET.

SALMON MAYONNAISE   POTTED SHRIMPS

NORWEGIAN ANCHOVIES   SOUSED HERRINGS

PLAIN & SMOKED SARDINES

ROAST BEEF

ROUND OF SPICED BEEF

VEAL & HAM PIE

VIRGINIA & CUMBERLAND HAM

BOLOGNA SAUSAGE   BRAWN

GALANTINE OF CHICKEN

CORNED OX TONGUE

LETTUCE   BEETROOT   TOMATOES

CHEESE.

CHESHIRE, STILTON, GORGONZOLA, EDAM,
CAMEMBERT, ROQUEFORT, ST. IVEL.
CHEDDAR

Iced draught Munich Lager Beer 3d. & 6d. a Tankard.

WHITE STAR LINE

TRIPLE SCREW STEAMER "TITANIC"

2ND CLASS

APRIL 11, 1912.

BREAKFAST.

FRUIT

ROLLED OATS   BOILED HOMINY

FRESH FISH

YARMOUTH BLOATERS

GRILLED OX KIDNEYS & BACON

AMERICAN DRY HASH AU GRATIN

GRILLED SAUSAGE, MASHED POTATOES

GRILLED HAM & FRIED EGGS

FRIED POTATOES

VIENNA & GRAHAM ROLLS

SODA SCONES

BUCKWHEAT CAKES, MAPLE SYRUP

CONSERVE   MARMALADE

TEA   COFFEE

WATERCRESS

WHITE STAR LINE.

R.M.S. "TITANIC."   APRIL 14, 1912.

THIRD   CLASS.

BREAKFAST.

OATMEAL PORRIDGE & MILK

SMOKED HERRINGS, JACKET POTATOES

HAM & EGGS

FRESH BREAD & BUTTER

MARMALADE   SWEDISH BREAD

TEA   COFFEE

DINNER.

RICE SOUP

FRESH BREAD   CABIN BISCUITS

ROAST BEEF, BROWN GRAVY

SWEET CORN   BOILED POTATOES

PLUM PUDDING, SWEET SAUCE

FRUIT

TEA.

COLD MEAT

CHEESE   PICKLES

FRESH BREAD & BUTTER

STEWED FIGS & RICE

TEA

SUPPER.

GRUEL   CABIN BISCUITS   CHEESE

Any complaint respecting the Food supplied, want of attention or incivility, should be at once reported to the Purser or Chief Steward. For purposes of identification, each Steward wears a numbered badge on the arm.

TITANIC MENUS (TITANIC: BLOOD AND STEEL)

The restaurant menus printed for the RMS Titanic's maiden voyage tell a story about the different qualities of service you might expect based on the ticket price you paid. In first class, you could dine on roast beef and chicken à la Maryland, washed down with tankards of ice-cold beer. In second class, Yarmouth bloaters and grilled ox kidneys are a treat. This particular menu was printed on the back of a blank postcard, so that you might send it to a friend when you docked (if you docked).

The caveat stamped on the bottom of the third-class menu—that you could report "any complaint respecting the Food supplied, want of attention or incivility"—might not fill you with confidence about the quality of the gruel and pickles you were about to receive or reassure you that, in the unlikely event of an emergency, it wouldn't be your lot who'd be left to drown below decks. The three replicas shown here were made without the printed photographs of the ship as they appear on the originals—we just didn't have the budget to pay the licensing fee.

SKETCH FOR PAWNBROKER'S SHOP WINDOW
(PENNY DREADFUL)

The hyphen breaking up "to-day" in the pawn-broker's shop window is a favorite antiquated spelling in English costume drama—it's a great example of how one tiny grammatical mark can make an entire street scene feel completely archaic. Abbreviated names, too, speak of a different time. Thomas was Thos, Mary was My, and George became Geo—shortened by tax collectors in a time when writing materials were precious, and writing with a dipping pen and nib was a slow, painstaking process. The abbreviations stuck and could be seen on hand-painted business signage throughout the nineteenth century. The word "holiday" can be found in texts dating as far back as the year 950, according to the Oxford English Dictionary, but "holy days" were still seen to be advertised as days off in the late 1800s.

These phrases might seem like small details in busy street scenes, but we can go smaller again: grammar and punctuation also speak of different times. The full stop at the end of the headings, dotted around most of these pieces of signage, is now almost completely antiquated. This seems to have been phased out of British publishing in the 1900s: a copy of the Times on Monday, August 12, 1929, shows periods at the end of its headlines; the next day, on Tuesday, it doesn't. It's fun to see an old-fashioned full stop in an old-fashioned graphic prop—it means someone, somewhere, is paying attention—but we won't lose any sleep over specific timelines. While these things can disappear from certain publications overnight, it could easily take another few decades for the convention to trickle down to every sign painter in town.

FOR WASHINGTON H'TS., THE BRONX AND QUEENS TRAINS
← TAKE LEFT ON EXIT

SPITTING
ON THE PLATFORMS OR OTHER
PARTS OF THIS STATION
IS
UNLAWFUL
OFFENDERS ARE LIABLE
TO ARREST

BY ORDER OF THE BOARD OF HEALTH

BMT LINES | BROAD ST

↑ EXIT TO STREETS | WA US

BROAD ST DOWNTO

WARNING DO NOT L

COURT ST. SUBWAY
UPTOWN to 59TH ST. & QUEENS
DOWNTOWN WHITEHALL ST. SOUTH FERRY
BROOKLYN and CONEY ISLAND

24HR SERV
B'KLN and Q
YOUR COU
IS APPREC

THIS SIDE FOR ——— NTOWN TRAINS

— THIS SIDE FOR ——— TOWN TRAINS

TER
HER

BROAD STREET MANHATTAN

JAMAICA NASSAU STREET

K DO NOT RUN ANDRAILS on STEP

DO NOT SMOKE
OR CARRY A LIGHTED
CIGARETTE, CIGAR OR
PIPE ON ANY STATION,
TRAIN, TROLLEY, OR BUS.

SPITTING
or **THROWING**
PAPERS OR OTHER LITTER
ON CAR OR STATION
FLOORS IS A VIOLATION
OF THE SANITARY CODE.

**OFFENDERS WILL BE
PROSECUTED.**

BOARD OF HEALTH   BOARD OF TRANSPORTATION
THE CITY OF NEW YORK

**N TO BAYRIDGE
3TH ST**

**BROOKLYN
MANHATTAN
TRANSIT**

AN OVER PLATFORM

**TO
ENS
ESY
ED**

**EXIT TO WILLIAM ST
FOR SERVICE TO NEW
LOTS AND FLATBUSH
LEXINGTON AV AND
BROADWAY EXPRESS**

CHAMBERS ST

CONEY ISLAND

6TH AVE

BROADWAY

DITMAS

NEW YORK SUBWAY SIGNS (BRIDGE OF SPIES) ← ←

Setting the period and the location of a story is an essential part of designing for film, but we can go a step further than that, using graphic language in set dressing to drive the narrative. Because Bridge of Spies opens with a chase sequence through 1950s Brooklyn, the production designer requested that one of the subway signs read WALK DO NOT RUN so that he could position it directly above the characters who were scripted to abruptly start running. This might seem subliminal—too subliminal, almost, to have been intentional—but everything we put in front of the camera is there for a reason. In this instance, the graphic design anticipates the scripted action, pushing the story forward, whether the audience is conscious of it or not.

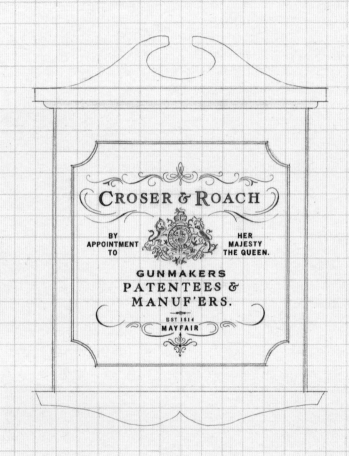

SKETCH FOR GUNMAKER'S SIGN (PENNY DREADFUL)

STREET POSTER: THE MATCHGIRLS' STRIKE
(PENNY DREADFUL)

Penny Dreadful's Victorian slum scenes were re-created around the Guinness Brewery district in Dublin, which is actually one of the nicer parts of the city now. It was almost unrecognizable when we shot the series, having been dressed down by the art department with great piles of rubble and shabby market stalls. The construction crew built large-scale fencing to hide any visible modern buildings, which we plastered with public service announcements warning the crowds of loitering, philandering, and the spread of incurable disease.

These street scenes were establishing shots— filmed from a crane high above the crowds to give a quick sense of the exterior location before cutting to the scripted action in the interior. It's unlikely that any street-poster artwork made the cut, but sometimes these things are designed purely to create an authentic world for the hundreds of extras to inhabit.

If standing around all day in a heavy costume and a light drizzle isn't enough to make you look suitably miserable, then maybe the thought of losing the lower half of your face to "phossy jaw" will help? A matchstick maker's occupational hazard, "phossy jaw" is the destruction of the jawbone resulting from overexposure to phosphorous—the white phosphorous tips of matches released a vapor that would rise up through the nostrils, building up deposits in the jaw over time. Toothaches and swollen gums would follow, then abscesses, with severely affected and exposed jawbones glowing neon green in the dark—eventually leading to brain damage and death by organ failure. The only known cure was to surgically remove the jaw. In 1888, the London Matchgirls' Strike sought to ban the use of white phosphorous, which then led the Salvation Army to open a matchstick factory that used only the comparatively safer red phosphorous instead.

Attention Matchgirls!

WE CALL FOR STRIKE!

TO-DAY, at 3 o'clock.

SEVENTEEN cases of 'Phossy Jaw' remain unreported by Matchstick Factory Owners. Phossy Jaw will TAKE YOUR JAW.

-------------- THERE IS --------------

NO KNOWN CURE.

Strike to be led by

Mrs. M. LEVERETT

of the

WOMEN'S TRADE UNION ASSOCIATION.

PHOSPHORUS IS A DANGER TO US ALL.

LIMEHOUSE HALL,
Bet. King St.
and Cinnamon St.,
Shadwell.

GOOD
SPEAKERS
will be
PRESENT.

BACKSTAGE SIGN (PENNY DREADFUL)

Rigging crews on large-scale theater productions were often made up of off-duty sailors, who used coded whistles to direct each other onboard their ships. Banning everyone else backstage from whistling meant that actors wouldn't be struck dead by someone unintentionally commanding a rig to be dropped on their heads.

As for peacock feathers, this particular ban was less practical: superstition said that the "evil eye" on the bird's tail feather was inexplicably responsible for actors forgetting their lines. This enamel piece, for the backstage area at Penny Dreadful's Grand Guignol theater, was painted onto new aluminum by our sign maker—who then drilled, filed, and painted its edges to give the impression of rusted old tin.

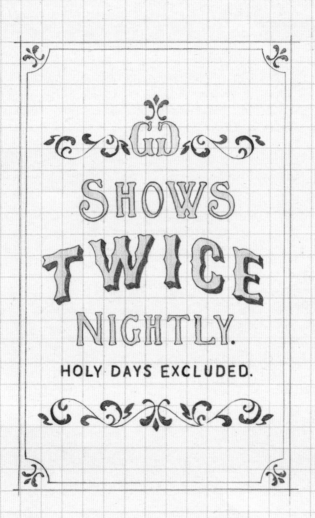

SHOWS
TWICE
NIGHTLY.
HOLY DAYS EXCLUDED.

SKETCH FOR THEATER SIGN (PENNY DREADFUL)

HOTEL MATCHBOX & STATIONERY
(BRIDGE OF SPIES)

It wasn't unusual during the mid-twentieth century for hotel stationery to promise a bath in every bedroom and to offer the slightly alarming assurance that the room you'd just checked into was "fireproof." Promises like this weren't really worth the paper they were printed on: in the event of an emergency, combustible interior paint and varnishes and the lack of multiple staircases made American hotels notoriously dangerous at this time. The Hotel Latham was the low-budget hotel where Rudolf Abel, the film's Russian spy, was living when the FBI caught him. The Hay-Adams, on the other hand, was located directly across from the White House and was where James Donovan, Abel's lawyer, stayed when he visited Washington, DC. Hotel-room scenes aren't necessarily always shot in hotels, but small pieces like these can help create the illusion of a real location.

200 Rooms   # Hotel Latham   200 Baths

FIREPROOF

Manhattan, New York

Value NAVEL ORANGES FOR 6/59¢ COHEN'S

HERMAN'S INC. UNIFORMS 28 ALTERATIONS WHILE YOU WAIT CLEANING & PRESSING

OWL AUTO SUPPLY Atlas TIRES AND BATTERIES IGNITION FUEL PUMP SERVICE

1253 COBBLE HILL CAPITOL ELECTRIC LIFE-SIZE TELEVISION BIG PICTURE T.V.

JENNINGS' MATCHLESS BAKING SODA FOR ALL PURPOSES

Knudsen FRESH MILK Good Teeth and Healthy Bones AT THE OLYMPIC GROCERY

ECONOMY BARBER SHOP HAIRCUT NOW ONLY $1 50¢ THIS WAY

LICHTENSTEIN & Co.

all TAILOR SUPPLIES & REMNANTS

LININGS WOOLENS MOHAIR
TRIMMINGS LINENS *muy barato!*

TODO PARA SASTRERIA 515-0198 CORTE PARA **PANTALONES**

GOODALL RUBBER CO. INC.

INDUSTRIAL RUBBER PRODUCTS

DECK HOSE	SEWER FLUSHING	METAL LINED HOSE	ACID PINCH VALVE
ACID HOSE	PAINT SPRAY HOSE	OXY-ACETYLENE	AUTOMOBILE RADIATOR
DUST EXHAUST	SAND BLAST HOSE	SYNPLASTIC	HOT WATER HOSE
CHIPPER AIR HOSE	SOLVENT	VACUUM AIR BRAKE	SEMI-METALLIC HOSE
FLUE CLEANER	STEAM CLEANING	VACUUM HOSE	SPRAY HOSE

TRY GOODALL WHEN YOUR NEXT INQUIRIES GO OUT. BRANCHES IN ALL PRINCIPAL CITIES.

LOEW'S KINGS THEATRE

1027 FLATBUSH AVENUE, BROOKLYN

THURS. FRI. NOV. 7-8

GRANT WILLIAMS · RANDY STUART

THE INCREDIBLE SHRINKING MAN

THE MOST INCREDIBLE STORY
THE SCREEN HAS EVER TOLD

Come on in, or smile as you pass!

NO U TURN — DEPT OF TRAFFIC

NO PARKING 8 AM TO 1 PM TUES. THURS. SAT. — DEPT OF TRAFFIC

5TH AV — WASHINGTON MEWS

AV OF THE AMERICAS — BROOME ST

E. 68 ST — F.D. ROOSEVELT DRIVE

FULTON — HUDSON AV

POLICE ONE-WAY DEPT

POLICE ONE-WAY DEPT

STREET SIGNAGE (BRIDGE OF SPIES) ← ←

When we shoot a film on location—out in the real world rather than on stages and in studio lots—much of the graphic work we make is needed to cover up existing modern signage and advertising on the streets. In superwide crane or drone shots, some of these pieces, like signs on rooftops, can be added later in post-production by the visual effects team, after we supply digital files. Down on the ground, entire blocks usually need to be dressed with physical graphic signage to create an authentic backdrop to the action, sometimes requiring hundreds of bespoke pieces to be manufactured just for a single scene.

It's important to check the little details in each of these pieces—you never know which signboard a character might be instructed to pause near as the director blocks out the scene. Spelling, anachronistic names, and pricing all need to be looked over with a fine-tooth comb. My first pass at the signage for the opening street scene of Bridge of Spies advertised economy haircuts at a barber shop for 25¢, which Adam Stockhausen, the production designer, immediately flagged: even for an economy cut, this sounded too cheap in 1957. I checked my references and he was right: the advert that I'd based it on was much older, a photograph taken in the 1930s. The film's art department assistant, Samuel Bader, did some research, and we changed the sign to $1.50—that extra dollar twenty-five would have made a considerable difference at the time.

CAFÉ MENU (PENNY DREADFUL)

"Decent but reasonable," our fictitious Metropole café took great pride in its lunch menu: the soup was "guaranteed hot," and the French coffee was "as served in Paris with one egg" (to the side, presumably). The grammatical error in the menu's dramatic opening line—"What are the wild wave's saying?"—was copied from a real reference. The "wild waves" were the people gossiping about how good the café's fare was, and the apostrophe was entirely redundant. I'd usually steer away from including mistakes like this, though. While it's worth noting that some of the world's greatest writers misused the apostrophe (Jane Austen used the possessive "it's" instead of "its," and Shakespeare pluralized "fellow's"), in general, apostrophe catastrophes in movie props should be avoided. No film graphic designer wants to be the butt of an angry letter to the Telegraph.

WHAT ARE THE
WILD WAVE'S SAYING?

In spite of all opposition Visitors declare
that the Best Place in Soho for
DECENT but REASONABLE luncheon is

THE
"Metropole"

1ᵈ	A POT of FRESH MADE TEA or COFFEE with Roll and Butter.	1ᵈ
2ᵈ	FRUIT TART or MILK PUDDING.	2ᵈ
7ᵈ	TEA or COFFEE with SHRIMPS and EGG & WATERCRESS, ad lib.	7ᵈ
3ᵈ	SMOKED MACKEREL with butter & one LARGE POTATO.	3ᵈ
6ᵈ	Plate of COLD MEAT or HAM with Bread and PICKLES.	6ᵈ
1ˢ	CUT from PRIME JOINTS with two VEGETABLES and BREAD.	1ˢ
1ˢ	LOIN CHOP or RUMP STEAK with two VEG. and BREAD.	1ˢ
7ᵈ	OYSTERS :- choicest brands served by the dozen.	7ᵈ
4ᵈ	FRENCH COFFEE as served in PARIS with ONE EGG.	4ᵈ
4ᵈ	BACON, per rasher.	4ᵈ
5ᵈ	TWO EGGS, with a BLOATER or a KIPPER.	5ᵈ
3ᵈ	SOUPS, all kinds, guaranteed HOT with BREAD.	3ᵈ
1ᵈ	PIPING HOT mug of CHOCOLATE.	1ᵈ
1ᵈ	GINGER BEER, LEMONADE, GLASS OF MILK, etc.	1ᵈ

OUR TEA IS UNSURPASSABLE AT 1/? PER CUP
BUT WE MAKE FOR ANY CUSTOMER FRESH AT 2/?

153

<u>SKETCHES FOR JAPANESE CHARACTERS</u>
(ISLE OF DOGS)

Drawing lettering in other languages is a challenge:
after nine months of working on Wes Anderson's
<u>Isle of Dogs</u>, I still wasn't exactly sure how the
three different Japanese alphabets worked.
Erica Dorn, the film's lead graphic designer,
would send me the text along with style sug-
gestions, and I would copy it by hand, carefully
drawing it up into pieces of signage, knowing
that any extra flourish I might add could inad-
vertently and completely change the meaning
of the words.

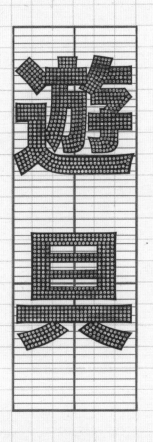

"RIDE"

"PAGODA SLIDE"

CHAPTER 6

<u>TOOLS</u>

FILMMAKING IS A TACTILE ENVIRONMENT, REQUIRING PHYSICAL
GRAPHIC DESIGN. WE TRY TO AVOID RE-CREATING GRAPHICS
DIGITALLY WHENEVER POSSIBLE, MAKING DIPPING PENS,
TYPEWRITERS, AND BOTTLES OF FAKE BLOOD STAPLES OF ANY
FILM GRAPHICS DEPARTMENT.

It didn't make sense to me, as a film graduate being called for an interview on The Tudors, that they would be looking for a full-time graphic designer on a series that was set in a time before graphic designers existed. I had seen several episodes of the show's first two seasons, and while I'd noticed the beautiful costume design and incredible set design, I hadn't really spotted any graphic design. The stained glass, maybe? Film school had taught me how to operate a camera, how to format a script, but it hadn't touched on graphic art. My advertising background—making web banners and logos and magazine spreads—seemed like it would be completely redundant on a costume drama set in the 1500s.

The move from commercial design to film design was a steep learning curve, and it didn't take me long to figure out that just because there were no graphic designers in the court of King Henry VIII didn't mean there wasn't any graphic design: it was just that, at that time, craftsmen produced the graphics. If the king wanted to chop his wife's head off, for example, he would need a death warrant, and if he needed a death warrant, he would need a calligrapher. In the 1500s, it was the scribe who was responsible for the layout of all the royal documents and their calligraphic styles; and today, in filmmaking, it's the graphic designer's job to imitate what they might have created, hiring a real calligrapher whenever necessary.

Nothing will ever seem as exciting to me now as that first season I spent at a film studio. It was a good summer for an Irish summer, and the studio lot was usually full of extras getting some sunshine while they waited for their next call. Servants, courtiers, knights, and princesses all smoking cigarettes and drinking coffee, standing around in their hats and corsets. Assistant directors buzzing about wearing headsets and walkie-talkies. Just the sight of a pair of stagehands carrying a throne across the parking lot was enough to fill me with a kind of unbridled joy. The movies! During one lunch break, the king of England smiled and said hello to me as I carried my tray across the canteen, and, not knowing how to respond, I had to stifle a kind of panicked curtsy. A curtsy!

The rest of the crew seemed indifferent to the actors. They called Jonathan Rhys Meyers "Johnny," and one night when we all went out in town, I saw a runner offer Joss Stone a potato chip as if it were absolutely nothing. I just wasn't good at talking to cast members, I decided. They seemed otherworldly to me, like aliens—extremely good-looking aliens—and I felt more comfortable hidden away in my graphics room, practicing tea staining and applying wax seals. Which was just as well because it turned out that I had a lot of practicing to do.

While I was able to draw on my commercial-design background for some aspects of the job—understanding the principles of layout design is an essential part of designing for any time period—I felt at a loss when it came to the craft of making actual physical, tactile hand props. Even the thought of putting in my first paper order felt overwhelming: What kind of stock would best double for parchment or vellum? Where would I find it? How much money should I be spending? Is my specialty printer paper about to break the entire budget of this $3-million-per-episode show?

It was clear, suddenly, that a masters degree in film production had taught me nothing about the practicalities of prop making—or budgeting—but luckily the show's departing graphic designer, Pilar Valencia, came back for some whirlwind training. Pilar knew everything there was to know about graphic set design and imitating old manuscripts, and she was encouraging and generous with her knowledge: over five short days, she gave me a complete crash course on everything from composing a script breakdown to using a feather quill. The week flew by—like all weeks at a film studio would come to—and on our last day together, as she left the art department, she patted my new desktop printer and said, "Now, this is your best friend." Her words didn't do much to help my rising sense of dread: operating uncooperative pieces of hardware just felt like another thing on the already quite long list of things I could see going wrong.

Still, there was something to be said for being thrown in the deep end, and my fascination with the work, for the most part, overshadowed any fear. I learned not to worry about breaking the budget: the tools and materials we need to make graphic props cost next to nothing compared to the necessary supplies of other members of the art department (building Hampton Court Palace, for example), and, as one scenic painter pointed out to me:

"You're better looking at it than looking for it." It would be a rookie mistake to leave myself short of any material when changes to props are so often requested at the very last minute, and my little graphics room became a cave of various paper types, threads, ribbons, beads, strings, and glues.

The show's production designer, Tom Conroy, took a hands-on approach to design, encouraging us to make things ourselves whenever possible, and the eagle-eyed set decorator, Crispian Sallis, instilled in me a new-found attention to detail. As the weeks went by, I found that there was an expert from every possible walk of life somewhere on a film set—whether you needed the advice of a carpenter or a dressmaker or a painter—and I spent much of my time down in the props workshop, where the model makers crafted the fixings for my scrolls, taught me how to stain paper, and made molds for the medals and coins that would eventually be painted to look like pieces of real gold.

It was all so far removed from the work I'd done in advertising, where I'd looked at a computer screen from the moment I'd arrived at my desk to the end of each working day. At a film studio, on a good day, graphic prop making felt more like play— all the things we'd made as children: the papier-mâché I'd made with my mother in the kitchen; the treasure maps we'd buried in the woods behind our back garden. I felt as if I'd found a job in a world that I'd heard about but had never really quite believed existed—like running away and joining a circus.

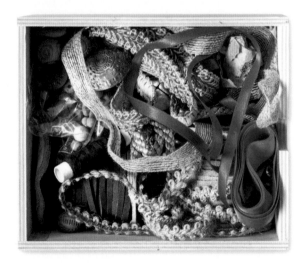

THREADS AND RIBBONS

Threads, ribbons, string, and other bits and
bobs used to dress graphic props, leftover
from the two seasons I spent on <u>The Tudors</u>.

Illustrious & most gracious Sovereign

I write faithfully to you on this day the twenty & sixth of Auguste, your Majesty, with news from the Courte of Kynge Henry the eyghth heir in Englaude. I wish that I had been able to w___ you prior, but I was struck again in my righte-hande with this dreaded gout so that, until yester-morning, I coulde not barely hold a pen.

Lord Winchester has lately been taken ill also, though not by the return of the sweating sickness as previously feared. Nevertheless, he had to disperse of his household and withdrawe to a house neare my own lodgings, and so there was opportunity to do him some civilities. On his arrival he came to dine with me, and, from an early houre until late, we conversed of public affaires, as of the Turks and the detestable practices of the Frenche. The following daye I invited Lord Winchester again to dinner, this time together with Secretary Vrisle, who is no less well inclined and has no less influence with the Kynge, and who was of the opinion that I shoulde take occasion to speak with the Kynge and repente his last persuasions, whiche woulde marvellously rebut the Frenche practices & advance those of the closer amity. And so on the sixteenthe I sent for audience, which was granted for the eighteenthe, when the Kynge received me a little more cordially than usual and thanked me for my affection to the closer amity & good offices, and said he was glad that things shoulde be treated by me, to whom

LEONEGRANCE

Treaty of Mu
of Englande
Againste the

It is agreed that the ancient and never interrupted alliance between Spaine and Englande shall not only be renewed and observed but shall likewise be made more strict by all other forts

✠

Jat datus hostiam puram hostiam fcain hosta umma culatu pane&fcin ute eterne ee crah tein salutis peaie le

fti angeli tuu m fubli me altare tuu ante confpm diuine maie statis tue et ysta ut qt quot ex hac altaris ofculteis altare parti

dignatus es m yucu tuu nisti o facraficiu putiu ma abuihe et o obtulit fumue dos tuus melch fein facticiu mn tu hostia cu mann dus Sip mus oin her yfeen at datus hostia puram hostia fcain hosta

King Henry VIII

TUDOR COLLECTION ← ←

Manuscripts, scrolls, and books from seasons
three and four of The Tudors.

KATHERINE HOWARD'S LETTER (THE TUDORS)

Finding the right calligrapher for a historical
drama can be tricky. Not only do they have
to be fluent in the various letterforms of the
period, but their hands also need to be of the
right gender, age, and skin tone: calligraphers
often have to stand in for cast members as hand
doubles. This can sound outlandish, especially
when we hear about actors performing all their
own sex scenes and horse-based stunts, but
passing as a professional scribe in close-up
can sometimes be a more complex undertaking.

The Irish calligrapher Gareth Colgan produced
some twenty different pieces for us on The
Tudors, in several different forms of writing—
all variations on Italic and Gothic cursive from
the era. Calligraphic styles are determined by
the place as well as the period: a document
written by an Italian character should look quite
different from one by the hand of an English-
man. I deferred to Gareth when it came to these
distinctions, as he has practiced calligraphy
since he was fourteen years old—working as
both a scribe and a letter carver in Cambridge,
England—and he could often be seen reading
some kind of heavy volume on the history of
paleography while waiting for his call to set.
Gareth's hands (male, white, midthirties) were
a good match for plenty of the characters on
The Tudors. He came to set five or six times over
the course of the series, always at the crack
of dawn along with the rest of the cast, and
was dressed each time in "half-costume." The
wardrobe department supplies all hand doubles
with the jacket and shirt of the actor they're
to stand in for—as well as any kind of large
feathered hat that might dangle into shot somehow—so that their cuffs are identical on camera.
(It doesn't matter how elaborate or historically
accurate a Tudor costume might be, jeans and
sneakers are entirely acceptable lower-half wear
for any calligraphy stand-in.)

The fourth season of The Tudors opened in the
middle of the great heat wave of 1539, with
a close-up of the French Ambassador Eustace
Chapuys writing home with the latest gossip
from court. The hot summer's day was illustrated in the script by the beads of sweat
rolling down Chapuys's forehead and onto the
letter in front of him. In this instance (our
summer might have been a good one but it
wasn't that good), Gareth had to work with
a prop man standing above him on a stepladder,
dropping water from a pipette as if it were
sweat falling from his brow. Chapuys was one
of the Tudor period's great chroniclers, known
for his extensive and detailed correspondence:
"I wish I had been able to write to you pryor,
but I was struck again in my righte hande with
this dreaded gout." His personal handwriting
style was bound to be on the more masterful end
of the scale, although we did ask Gareth to make
it look even more elegant than may have been
historically correct: we wanted a nice contrast between the exquisite lettering and the
squashed fly that Chapuys was scripted to swat
dead. (Gareth's hands were also playing the role
of fly swatter: the props team had collected
a whole tin of dead bluebottles for him, to allow
for a number of takes, if necessary.)

Not all of a show's characters are masters
of penmanship, though. The real-life Henry
VIII's handwriting was particularly tough
to decipher, and his on-screen persona's
scrawled list of potential suitors had to be
modernized by the calligrapher to make it more
legible to a contemporary television audience.
Henry's fifth wife, the teenager Katherine
Howard, was said by some historians to have
been almost illiterate, which we exaggerated
for dramatic effect in the television series
when we showed her penning a frantic letter
to her (alleged) boyfriend Thomas Culpeper:
"Master Coulpeper, I hertely recomend me unto
youe praying you to sende me worde how that
yo doo." Katherine's letter is thought to have
been the evidence that the king needed to con-
firm her death sentence, and she was beheaded
at the Tower of London when she was just nine-
teen years old.

It was our art department trainee, Megan
Breslin, who was drafted to play the young
queen's hands, and, like Gareth playing the
hands of Chapuys before her, she would also
get her own prop man with a pipette on a stepladder—although this time it was to create
the tears falling from her face. Despite having
naturally very neat handwriting—and being
pretty adept at using a quill—there were two
key factors that made Megan's writing beautifully manic. One, she wrote the letter with her
right hand instead of her usual left, and two,
she was so nervous that as soon as she was
in costume and taken to set, her hands began
to shake uncontrollably.

Master Culpeper I hertely
recommend me vnto youe
praying you to sende me
worde how that yo doo It
was shewed me that you was
seke the wyche thynge trobled
me very muche tell suche
tyme that I here from you
praying you to send me worde
how that you do for I
never longed so muche for
thynge as I do to se you
and to speke wyth you
the wyche I trust shall
be shortely nowe the wyche
dothe comforthe me verre
muche whan I thynk of

good vnto that pore felowe my
man wyche is on of the grefes
that I do departe from hym
for then I do know noone that
I dare truste to sende to you
and therfor I pray you take
hym to be wyth you that I may
be mynde here from you one
thynge I pray you to gyue me
a horse frome my man for I
had muche a do to get
one and therfore I pray sende
me one by hym and yo so
doyng I am as I sade afar and
thus I take my leve of you
trustyng to se you shortely
agayne and wans thynke agayne

that you shall departe
from me a gayne ytt makes
my harte to dye to thynk
what fortune I have that
I cannot be always yn your
company yt my trust is
always in you that you
wolde us yn have promysed
me and in that hope I
truste vpon styll prayeng
yow that that you will you
tha my lade Rochforde
here for then I shalla bede
of lengar to be as your
commandment Thaydyng
gou for that you have
promysed me to be so

yt was wythe me now
that you mente se wad payn
I take yn wrytyng to you.

yours as long as
lyffe endures

Katheryn

one thyng I had forgotten
and that is to instruct my man
to tarie here wyth me still
for he says whatsomever you
bed hym will do yt and

1 Lady Jane Askew
2 Cathererine of Ascham
3 Katherine Ashley
4 Anne Stuart
5 Lady Camilla of York
6 Margaret Parry
7 Blanche Spencer
8 Annabella Spencer
9 Anne Spencer
10 Elizabeth Willoughby
11 Elizabeth Cecil
12 Lady Catherine Courtenay
13 Elizabeth Marlowe
14 Mary Dudley
15 Lady Jane Denny
16 Lady Victoria Throckmorton
17 Lady Dru Throckmorton
18 Marie de Beaufort
19 Lady Ursula Hardwick
20 Anne Hilliard
21 Jane Hilliard
22 Mary Hepburn
23 Eugenia Latimer
24 Charlotte Paget
25 Beatrice Radcliffe
26 Lady Catherine de Boise

STAINING AND AGING PAPER → →

(1) No aging (2) Tea (3) Bleach and lemon juice
(4) Brasso Polish (5) Potassium permanganate
crystals (6) Coffee (7) Balsamic vinegar,
cooked in the oven for ten minutes (8) Red
wine vinegar (9) Burnt with match

There's nothing quite as satisfying as sinking
a piece of crisp white paper into a tray of tea
and watching it turn a lovely antique brown.
Tea staining is a staple of art departments,
used to make piles of paperwork look old.
It also makes the paper look like it was once
dropped in a puddle, so we have to choose
the right stock and give everything a good iron
to try to flatten things back out again. (Some
coated papers will never flatten properly again,
but handmade textured papers absorb water well
without any crinkling.)

Tea can be substituted with instant coffee
granules—if you're working in a country outside Ireland or the UK where cheap, stringless
teabags are less readily available. The color
is comparatively the same, although the result
is a much lighter stain that requires a longer
steep. Lemon juice can strip the color from
some darker papers, making them look blotchy
and sun bleached. Actual bleach can take that
even further—just don't let it soak too long.
Potassium permanganate crystals can create
a sprinkled, stained effect; burnt edges immediately conjures up a pirate ship.

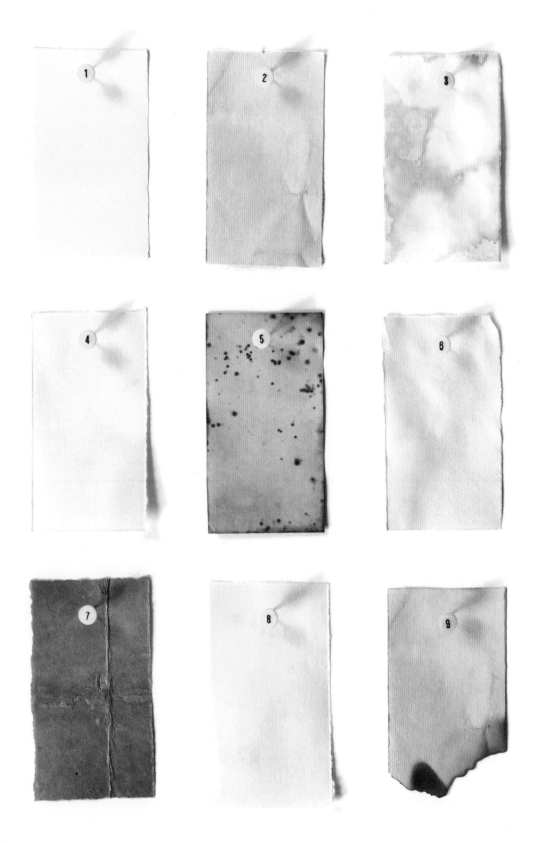

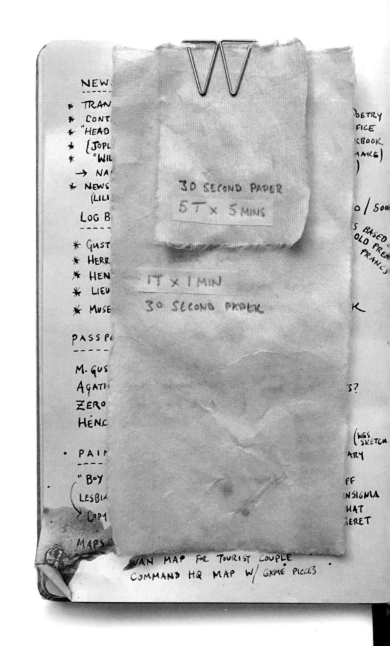

NEW.
* TRAN
* CONT
* "HEAD
* {JOPL
* "WIL
→ NA
* NEWS
  (LILI

LOG B

* GUST
* HERR
* HEN
* LIEU
* MUSE

PASSP

M. GUS
AGATH
ZERO
HENC

• PAIN

" BOY
(LESBI
→ COPY

MAPS

POETRY
FICE
KBOOK
AAKE)
)

0 / 500

S BASED
OLD FREN
FRANCS

K

3?

(WES
SKETCH
ARY

FF
NSIGNIA
HAT
SERET

AN MAP FOR TOURIST COUPLE
COMMAND HQ MAP W/ GAME PIECES

30 SECOND PAPER
5 T × 5 MINS

IT × I MIN
30 SECOND PAPER

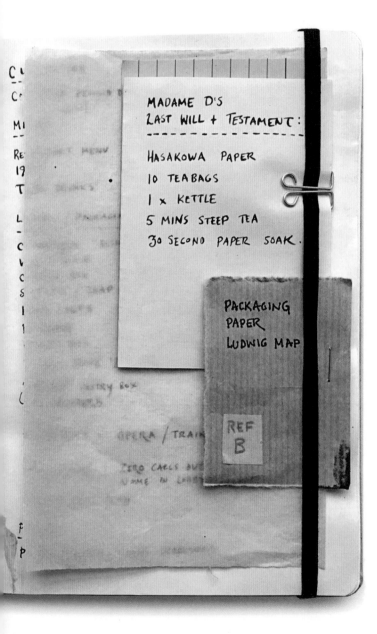

MADAME D'S
LAST WILL + TESTAMENT:
- - - - - - - - - - - - - - - - -
HASAKOWA PAPER
10 TEABAGS
1 x KETTLE
5 MINS STEEP TEA
30 SECOND PAPER SOAK.

PACKAGING
PAPER
LUDWIG MAP

REF
B

TEA-STAINING RECIPES ← ←

The key to staining paper is to experiment for each individual prop, keeping a careful log of recipes. If we're called to remake a document for a reshoot, continuity of tone can be tricky if we don't have ratios and timings written down. An old recipe pictured here used for staining a last will and testament, a document that was meant to look like it was written in 1886, calls for ten tea bags steeped in one kettle of water for five minutes.

Of course, not every document in a period movie needs to be aged: many of the pieces we make are supposed to be brand new in a script's storyline. Still, giving graphic props a slight patina can help convince an audience that they belong to a different time—and weren't actually printed in a film's art department the day before the shoot.

FAKE BLOOD

When fake blood was first sold in bottles, the color was all-important—bright red concoctions were mixed especially for theater audiences. When the movies arrived, the tone of the blood became more important—black-and-white film-makers are said to have used chocolate syrup to achieve a starker contrast on camera. Today, you can buy different tones and consistencies for different needs—fresh bright blood, running blood, oozing blood, or thick dark blood, depending on the action—or you can just mix it yourself, using a recipe of corn syrup and food coloring. Applying blood to graphics is usually the responsibility of the props team— on The Grand Budapest Hotel, it was the on-set stand by prop man, Till Sennhenn, who stained each telegram, using several different kinds for a layered effect and drying it with a hot air gun to congeal it. Still, it's handy to have a bottle or two in the graphics department: you never know when a director might request a quick preview of how a graphic might look with a splash of red across it.

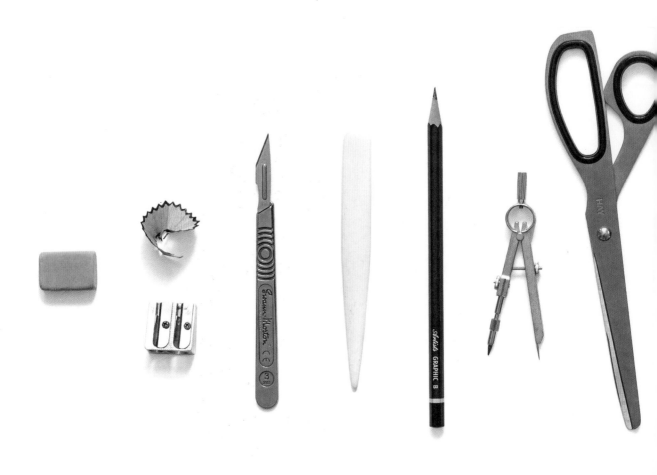

BASIC KIT

The question I'm asked most often when I teach a workshop in graphic prop making is: What tools do I need in my kit? It's hard to give a satisfying answer. The tools you'd need for a story set during the gold rush are probably quite different to what you might need on a spaceship, and any kit will accumulate organically over time. (I have more sticks of sealing wax now than is really necessary, all leftover from my days on The Tudors.) Aside from all the computer

equipment—laptops, scanners, screens, printers, hard drives—the best tools you can arm yourself with at first are a basic pencil case, with good pencils, fresh scalpel blades, a measuring tape, and a pen that you love to draw with. Pictured above, from left to right: eraser, pencil sharpener, scalpel, folding bone, pencil, compass, scissors, steel rule, dipping pen, hole punches, red sealing wax, tape measure, dipping ink, and a needle and thread.

PINK MEASURING TAPE

One of the best tips I've ever received regarding
my kit came from the supervising art director
on <u>Vikings</u>, Carmel Nugent. She suggested I
paint my measuring tape with bright pink nail
polish to deter anyone in the construction
crew from walking off with it by mistake.

TEENAGE DIARY (METAL HEART)

When we design for film, we're not always designing as graphic designers; instead, we have to step into the shoes of the movie's characters. In Metal Heart (dir. Hugh O'Conor, 2018) twins Emma and Chantal couldn't be less alike: at sixteen, Chantal is a successful businesswoman and social media influencer, while her twin is a daydreamer in a band that has never had a gig. Emma's diary was scripted to be full of her lyrics, thoughts, and doodles.

What would a sixteen-year-old goth have used to draw with? We settled on a cheap black ballpoint pen and Tipp-Ex (similar to Wite-Out). Later, the production designer, Neill Treacy, showed the doodles in the notebook to the scenic artist, Alan Lambert, asking him to paint them onto the surfaces of Emma's bedroom, as if she had spent her entire adolescence drawing all over her ceiling and walls.

PAPER FASTENINGS

The right fastening can be the finishing touch to a graphic prop, although we have to be careful not to use anything that seems anachronistic. The first known stapler, for example, was made as early as the 1700s, for King Louis XV in France, but the cost of the pure gold staples and the tedium of having to reload each one meant that the device didn't come into popular usage until George McGill reinvented it in the 1870s. (It seems that McGill had dedicated much of his life's work to the fastening together of documents, having previously invented the ever-useful brass split pin some years before.)

Treasury tags—short lengths of string with metal crosspieces at each end—first appear on record in a list of items published by Her Majesty's Stationery Office in 1912, replacing the makeshift waxed ribbons used to bind paperwork together. The first paper clip, invented in 1899 by the Norwegian Johan Vaaler, was apparently issued in a range of different shapes at first, the abstract on its patent reading, "a piece of wire, that is bent to a rectangular, triangular, or otherwise-shaped hoop, the end parts of which wire piece form members or tongues lying side-by-side in contrary directions."

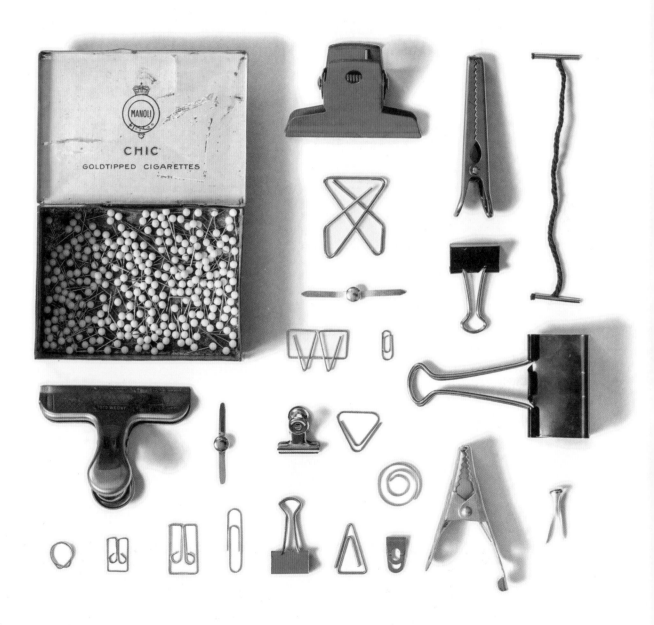

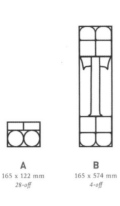

STAINED

Stained Glass leading
3mm MDF; paint

Fixed to Perspe
Cathedral gl

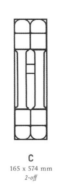
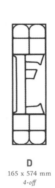
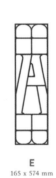

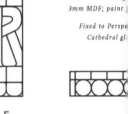

A	**B**	**C**	**D**	**E**	**F**	
165 x 122 mm	165 x 574 mm	165 x 574 mm	165 x 574 mm	165 x 574 mm	165 x 574 mm	122 x
28-off	4-off	2-off	4-off	2-off	2-off	

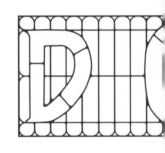

M
1498 x 574 mm
1-off

CERAMIC TILES
Patterned tiles to be printed on vinyl;
Fixed to MDF pieces;
Paint finish as ceramic with scored grout lines.

Q	**R**	**V**	**S**	**T**	**U**
115 x 122 mm	126 x 122 mm	190 x 122 mm	126 x 574 mm	115 x 574 mm	190 x 574 mm
4-off	8-off	8-off	4-off	2-off	4-off

NB. COLOUR OVERVIEW N.T.S.

Perspex to be painted as Stained Glass with French enamel:

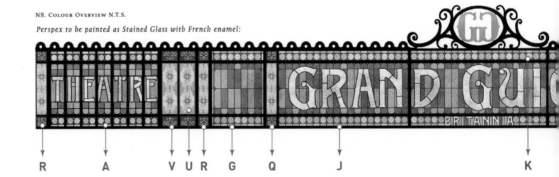

R	A	V	U	R	G	Q	J	K

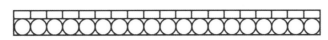

J
1498 x 122 mm
4-off

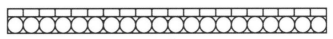

K
1560 x 122 mm
1-off

L
1560 x 122 mm
1-off

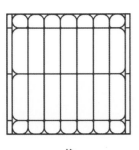

H
574 x 605 mm
2-off

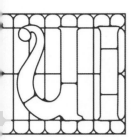

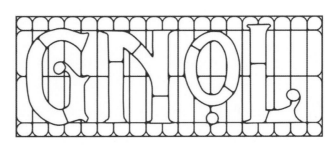

P
1498 x 574 mm
1-off

W
1586 x 492 mm
1-off
Mild Steel painted as Black Cast Iron

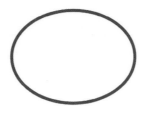

X
610 x 454 mm
2-off
6mm MDF painted as Black Cast Iron

Y
6483 x 626 mm
1-off
6mm MDF painted as Gold Cast Iron

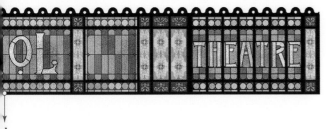

PENNY DREADFUL				
PRODUCTION DESIGNER: JONATHAN McKINSTRY				
SET	Grand Guignol Theatre Ext.		LOC	Dame Lane
DETAIL	Canopy Graphics		DWG. № 553 *(To be read with № 533)*	REV
DRAWN AA	DATE 30.1.14	SET № 3.44	SCALE 20%	
PROD	CARPS X	PROPS	PASSED BY J. McKinstry	
DIR	PLAST	LOC		
CAM	PAINT X	SFX	ISSUED ON 30.1.14	
ELEC	RIGGS	VIS FX		
ART	METAL X	GRAPHICS X	REVISED ON	
C.M X	SET DEC X	SIGNWTR X		

GRAND GUIGNOL THEATER FRONTAGE
(PENNY DREADFUL) ← ←

As I began to work on productions set in different periods and places, I established a rule for myself: if something was made by hand at the time, then I would make it by hand now. I had found that trying to make digital fonts look like hand lettering was unnecessarily time consuming: it was easier and more effective to just pick up a pencil and start drawing.

In Penny Dreadful's third episode, based largely in and around the Grand Guignol theater in Victorian London's Soho district, we're introduced to Vincent Brand, "an actor-manager of the most orotund manner...late middle age, given to paunch he inadequately conceals in all manner of flamboyant waistcoats." Brand is, as the screenwriter, John Logan, described in the script: "so rare for this story, immediately likeable." The production designer, Jonathan McKinstry, stipulated that the Grand Guignol theaterfrontage should be an extension of Brand's own character: colorful, flamboyant, and charming.

We could have used a typeface for the theater's lettering—there are plenty of art deco styles like this available to download from font libraries. But the rule about making things by hand came into its own here: the stained-glass execution of the sign meant that its lettering would have been drawn and cut by the glazier in reality, without them necessarily ever having seen the font. (Note, also, that the "G" shape in the cast-iron piece at the top of the sign is completely different from those in the glass lettering, which would have been designed by the blacksmith.)

Drawing the letters and patterns by hand in the glass and tiles gave each one a more organic feel and meant that no two letters were exactly the same. Eventually, the drawings were digitized, scanned, and imported into Adobe Illustrator, which I used to trace and vectorize each piece in order to make a scale working drawing for the glazier and metalworkers. The art directors decided, though, that the glass elements should actually be made out of acrylic: the piece would be situated over the actors' heads, and lighter and safer material was preferable. (Similarly, the cast-iron metalwork was actually shaped from steel.) The painters are able to make these things look like different materials: for example, painting the plastic with PVA glue to produce a mottled, stained-glass effect and adding rust and flakes to the metalwork.

Our very first introduction to Brand was a shot of him peeing drunkenly in an alleyway, and it suited the tone of the script that the lettering in the theater sign was very slightly irregular rather than typed. "There is a place where the malformed find grace," Brand says as he introduces the building to the show's audience. "Where the hideous can be beautiful. Where strangeness is not shunned but celebrated. This place is the theater."

EMBOSSING TAPE LETTERING

This distinctively industrial lettering is made with a handheld label maker and embossing tape. It was invented by Dymo in 1958, but the tool pictured here isn't all that different, bought brand new in 2011 for a 1970s-themed advertisement that I worked on. The machine features the whole Roman alphabet and ten numbers (and some limited punctuation), and the tape comes in a range of colors—although I usually stick to red or black if the movie is based on themes of espionage. The text is always white: it's the stretching of the plastic that displays the characters, rather than any kind of applied pigment.

TOP SECRET

ESPIONAGE

CONFIDENTIAL

CLASSIFIED

INDEX

53.3493N. 6.2603W

ATARI'S STENCILED EMBLEM (ISLE OF DOGS)

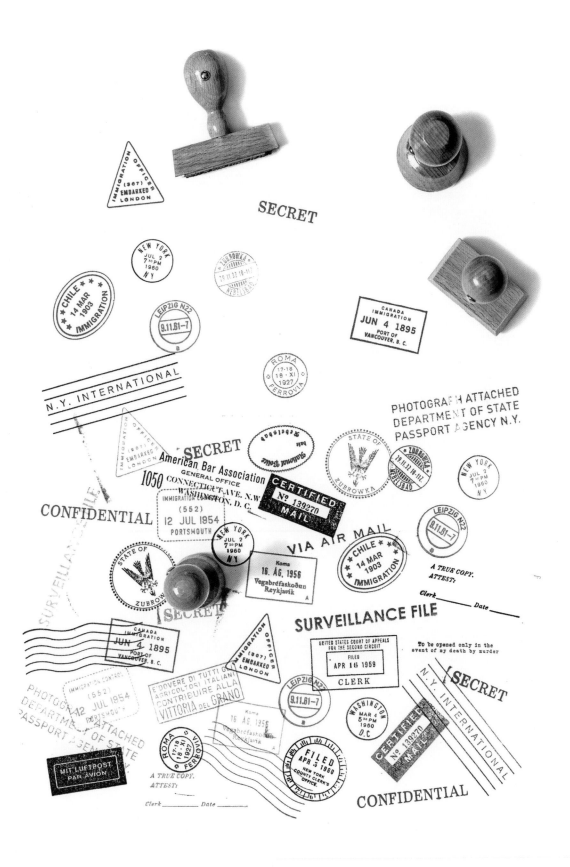

VARIOUS RUBBER STAMPS

LINOCUT LETTERS FOR THE TRASH ISLAND DECREE
(ISLE OF DOGS)

I could spend all day working in Photoshop,
trying to distress a digital "stamp" to make
it look like it was applied to a document with
inked rubber. But it's much easier and more
effective to get the real stamp made—the same
goes for stenciling, spray-painting, and linocut
lettering. While there are all kinds of digital
brushes and distressed fonts available to create
effects like these, nothing says "made by hand"
like actually making things by hand—and there's
still at least one rubber stamp maker in every
big town. (We try to find stamps made with
wooden rather than plastic handles whenever we
can. One prop master I worked for pointed out
that they can be handy for use in action, when
background extras play hotel receptionists or
office clerks. Extras always need something to
do with their hands, to stop them from slumping
over like zombies by the end of a long shooting day—and the wooden handle doesn't date
a stamp like plastic can.)

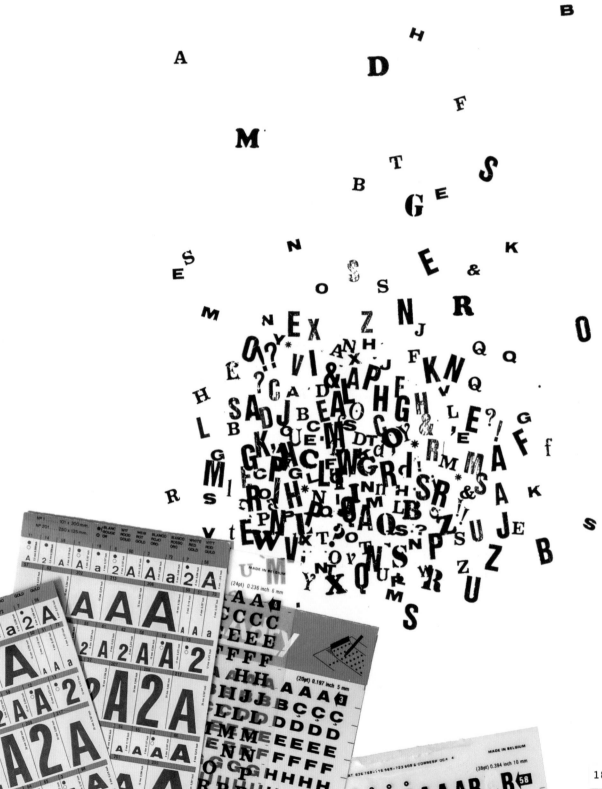

DRY-TRANSFER LETTERING

If graphic design for film sometimes feels more like play than work, then nothing feels more like play than the application of dry-transfer lettering: alphabetized decals on thin plastic sheets that can be rubbed onto the surface of a movie prop.

The process sounds like it was more tedious when it was literally the only option available. My father, Bruce Atkins, trained as a graphic designer in the 1960s, started setting type with transfers at design school, and, although it was increasingly replaced by digital typesetting bromides, he continued to use it right up until the first Apple Mac typesetter arrived at the design agency he worked at in the 1980s.

In the early days, Letraset was used as the original artwork, ready to be photographed directly onto film to make the printing plate.

This process evolved into what my father now describes as "a simple, standard artwork workflow," in which they (a) hand sketched the layout to determine type content and sizes; (b) chose the type style and fetched the relevant lettering sheet; (c) rubbed down the words; (d) photographed the layout; (e) exposed, processed, and made up a black-and-white bromide of the words at full artwork size; and finally, (f) cut and pasted up the artwork (literally cutting and pasting artwork) using repositionable rubber cement. He remembers half-used sheets of Letraset littered all over the floor of the London studio where he worked; the letters that they most frequently needed were always missing. Sometimes he would bring these sheets home with him as a treat, and I would scratch the remaining letters into my notebooks, making patterns with the strange punctuation, and rows of "Qs" and "Xs" and "Zs."

THREE TYPEWRITERS → →

Different typewriters use different fonts. It's preferable to use a machine that's chronologically appropriate to the period of the script when possible, but we're not complete sticklers. This beautiful red Olivetti Valentine was lent to me by a family friend to use on <u>Bridge of Spies</u>— although the Valentine was actually made in 1968, ten years after the events of the script. Still, the type style wasn't overtly anachronistic, and the more important consideration was that the typewritten notes didn't look like they were created with a digital font. While there are some great fonts available that have been lifted directly from scans of real type, it can be more effective just to bang out these notes on an analog machine, with all the natural anomalies you'd expect to find in a document typed by hand: some keys occasionally pressed heavier than others, some not pressed heavily enough, and certain letters offset from the baseline. (Think of all the midcentury murder mysteries solved by a repeatedly raised "T" in the villain's correspondence.) When we do use a digital font in place of a real typewriter—usually in background dressing rather than in hero props— it helps to have an original typewritten sheet to check the printed scale: we want to avoid suggesting that we used a typewriter with an impossibly enormous eighteen-point font size.

<u>OLIVETTI VALENTINE</u> (1968, NICKNAMED "THE PORTABLE RED")

SHARK ATTACK

OLIVETTI DORA (1974)

SHARK ATTACK

FACIT TP2 (1968)

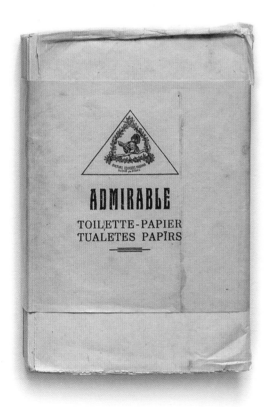

ADMIRABLE

TOILETTE-PAPIER
TUALETES PAPĪRS

When I was working on a spy movie set during World War II (the working title was, coincidentally, Miss Atkins's Army), I received a strangely well-timed email from a man in Latvia named Janis Linde, who said he had a large batch of slightly yellowed 1940s paper for sale. Naturally aged paper is like gold dust in a film graphics department—while staining and ironing paper can be effective for certain props, there's always the impression that the paper was once wet or even water-logged. On The Grand Budapest Hotel, the property buyer, Eckart Friz, gave our graphics department three large boxes of paper salvaged from old East German Stasi offices: pale pinks and greens and yellows, each sheet's edges slightly discolored from exposure but in otherwise perfect condition. We used some pages for printing hero props—it was too precious, really, for use in background dressing—and we had some left over for Bridge of Spies, which we almost completely used up.

Janis told me that he had found his collection of old paper almost twenty years ago, when he was renovating the small garden house at his family home. He'd noticed that one of the building's outer walls was much thicker than the others, and when he knocked it down, he found a secret hollow filled with stacks upon stacks of packages, all carefully wrapped in large sheets of wartime black-out paper for windows. Inside each package was reams of unused paper—lined paper, graph paper, blotting paper, music manuscript paper— as well as unopened boxes of pencils, pens, notebooks, ledger books, and all kinds of other stationery and office supplies, in near pristine condition.

Janis remembered that his great-grandfather Hermanis Upens had owned a stationery shop in Riga in the 1940s. Janis had written with pencils from the shop as a child and played with boxes of the shop's branded playing cards. Stationery retail was a fairly industrious trade at a time when paper was often the most essential tool in any working day, and Hermanis kept his shop stocked full with goods from the large paper mill on the Līgatne River, close to the Russian border. It was a small family business, but a busy one: his wife, Elvira, ran the counter while he managed all back-end operations. Their livelihood was seized, like most privately owned businesses, when the Soviet Union occupied Latvia during World War II. Janis's great-grandparents were tipped off about the impending nationalization and advised to willingly hand over their store and all its goods—the only way to save themselves from deportation to labor camps. They managed to hide some of their stationery in the hollow wall of their garden house before everything was taken away from them. The Soviet occupation lasted almost fifty years, and Latvia's sovereignty wasn't fully restored until 1991. Hermanis and Elvira were never permitted to return to their business.

Janis found their stash—like uncovering treasures, he said—in the 1990s, but it would be twenty years or more before it occurred to him that it might be useful to somebody, somewhere, for something. When he started his own business (building motion sensors for sports), he decided to reach out to film designers to see if selling this paper for use in movie props might help fund his new venture. I immediately bought a selection of stock from him, and I know that many of my colleagues working on various film projects around the world did, too. It's strange to think that Hermanis and Elvira Upens will never know what happened to their hidden wares: that seventy years later, their great-grandson was able to finance his own business because of them, and every now and then a sheet of their paper gets a close-up in a movie, as a hero prop.

IMAGE CREDITS

DIMENSIONS ARE GIVEN IN

HEIGHT X WIDTH X DEPTH

INTRODUCTION

PROTEST SIGNAGE
placards ¾ × 1⅓ in. (2 × 3 cm)
Isle of Dogs (dir. Wes Anderson, 2018)
Production Designers: Paul Harrod &
Adam Stockhausen
Graphic Designer: Annie Atkins
Assistant Graphic Designer: Molly Rosenblatt
Photograph by Flora Fricker
"ISLE OF DOGS" © 2018 Twentieth Century Fox.
All rights reserved.

ZOLTAR'S CARD
2 × 3½ in. (5 × 8.9 cm)
Big (dir. Penny Marshall, 1988)
Production Designer: Santo Loquasto
Set Decorators: George DeTitta Jr. &
Susan Bode-Tyson
Graphic Designer unknown
"BIG" © 1988 Twentieth Century Fox.
All rights reserved.

THE TIMES (LONDON, 1945)
24 × 18 in. (61 × 45.7 cm)
Photograph by Flora Fricker
Courtesy The Times / News Licensing

CHAPTER 1

THE GREAT BIG BOOK OF WHEELS AND WINGS
cover 16 × 11 in. (40.6 × 27.9 cm)
Bridge of Spies (dir. Steven Spielberg, 2015)
Production Designer: Adam Stockhausen
Set Decorator: Rena DeAngelo
Property Master: Sandy Hamilton
Graphic Designer: Annie Atkins
Photograph by Flora Fricker
"BRIDGE OF SPIES" © 2015 Twentieth Century
Fox. All rights reserved. Courtesy of
Storyteller Distribution Co., LLC.

WEST GERMAN FOOD PACKAGING
sugar for scale 5½ × 4 × 2 in.
(14 × 10.2 × 5 cm)
Bridge of Spies (dir. Steven Spielberg, 2015)
Production Designer: Adam Stockhausen
Set Decorator (Germany): Bernhard Henrich
Property Master (Germany): Eckart Friz
Graphic Designers: Annie Atkins &
Liliana Lambriev
Photograph by Flora Fricker
"BRIDGE OF SPIES" © 2015 Twentieth Century
Fox. All rights reserved. Courtesy of
Storyteller Distribution Co., LLC.

LETTERING SKETCH FOR MILK CARTON
11½ × 8 in. (29.2 × 20.3 cm)
Bridge of Spies (dir. Steven Spielberg, 2015)
Production Designer: Adam Stockhausen
Set Decorator: Rena DeAngelo

Graphic Designer: Annie Atkins
"BRIDGE OF SPIES" © 2015 Twentieth Century
Fox. All rights reserved. Courtesy of
Storyteller Distribution Co., LLC.

PASSPORT
6 × 3½ in. (15.2 × 8.9 cm)
Bridge of Spies (dir. Steven Spielberg, 2015)
Production Designer: Adam Stockhausen
Set Decorator: Rena DeAngelo
Property Master: Sandy Hamilton
Property Master (Germany): Eckart Friz
Graphic Designers: Annie Atkins &
Liliana Lambriev
Photograph of Tom Hanks as James Donovan
by Jaap Buitendijk
Photograph of passport by Flora Fricker
"BRIDGE OF SPIES" © 2015 Twentieth Century
Fox. All rights reserved. Courtesy of
Storyteller Distribution Co., LLC.

BOYS' MAGAZINE SPREAD, 1950s
11 × 16 in. (27.9 × 40.6 cm)
Bridge of Spies (dir. Steven Spielberg, 2015)
Production Designer: Adam Stockhausen
Set Decorator: Rena DeAngelo
Property Master: Sandy Hamilton
Graphic Designer: Annie Atkins
Photograph by Flora Fricker
"BRIDGE OF SPIES" © 2015 Twentieth Century
Fox. All rights reserved. Courtesy of
Storyteller Distribution Co., LLC.

BULLET HOLES
1–3 in. (2.5–7.6 cm) diameter
Bridge of Spies (dir. Steven Spielberg, 2015)
Production Designer: Adam Stockhausen
Art Director (Germany): Marco Bittner Rosser
Graphic Designers: Liliana Lambriev &
Annie Atkins
Photograph by Flora Fricker
"BRIDGE OF SPIES" © 2015 Twentieth Century
Fox. All rights reserved. Courtesy of
Storyteller Distribution Co., LLC.

THE AMERICAN MUSEUM OF NATURAL HISTORY
FLOOR TILES
1,200 sq. ft. (366 sq. m)
Wonderstruck (dir. Todd Haynes, 2017)
Production Designer: Mark Friedberg
Art Director: Kim Jennings
Assistant Art Director: Michael Auszura
Graphic Designers: Edward A. Ioffreda &
Annie Atkins
Courtesy of Amazon Content Services LLC

ESPIONAGE DOCUMENTS
various sizes: see ruler for scale
Bridge of Spies (dir. Steven Spielberg, 2015)
Production Designer: Adam Stockhausen
Set Decorator: Rena DeAngelo
Set Decorator (Germany): Bernhard Henrich
Property Master: Sandy Hamilton

Property Master (Germany): Eckart Friz
Graphic Designers: Annie Atkins &
Liliana Lambriev
Photograph by Flora Fricker
"BRIDGE OF SPIES" © 2015 Twentieth Century
Fox. All rights reserved. Courtesy of
Storyteller Distribution Co., LLC.

EIGHTEEN MAPS
2 x 2 in. (5 x 5 cm)
Isle of Dogs (dir. Wes Anderson, 2018)
Production Designers: Paul Harrod &
Adam Stockhausen
Graphic Designer: Annie Atkins
Assistant Graphic Designer: Chinami Narikawa
Photograph by Flora Fricker
"ISLE OF DOGS" © 2018 Twentieth Century Fox.
All rights reserved.

U-2 PILOT COCKPIT DOCUMENTS
folded maps 6 x 4 in. (15.2 x 10.1 cm)
map with yellow stickers 11 x 6 in.
(27.9 x 15.2 cm)
green document 7½ x 4 in. (19 x 10.2 cm)
Bridge of Spies (dir. Steven Spielberg, 2015)
Production Designer: Adam Stockhausen
Property Master: Sandy Hamilton
Property Master (Germany): Eckart Friz
Set Decorator: Rena DeAngelo
Graphic Designers: Annie Atkins &
Liliana Lambriev
Photograph by Flora Fricker
"BRIDGE OF SPIES" © 2015 Twentieth Century
Fox. All rights reserved. Courtesy of
Storyteller Distribution Co., LLC.

SKETCHES OF BOX LABELS
11½ x 8 in. (29.2 x 20.3 cm)
The Boxtrolls (Laika, dir. Graham Annable &
Anthony Stacchi, 2014)
Production Designers: Michel Breton,
August Hall, Paul Lasaine & Tom McClure
Art Director: Curt Enderle
Graphic Designers: Josh Holtsclaw &
Annie Atkins
Reproduced by permission of Laika LLC
© 2012 Laika. All Rights Reserved.

CINEMA TICKETS
1 x 2 in. (2.5 x 5 cm)
Wonderstruck (dir. Todd Haynes, 2017)
Production Designer: Mark Friedberg
Set Decorator: Debra Schutt
Property Master: Sandy Hamilton
Graphic Designer: Annie Atkins
Photograph by Flora Fricker
Courtesy of Amazon Content Services LLC

LONDON ZOO
each sign 12-40 in. high, 24-60 in. wide
(30.5-101.6 cm high, 60.9-152.4 cm wide)
monkey info 13 x 24 in. (33 x 61 cm)
Please Do Not Encourage the Monkeys sign

8 x 13 in. (20.3 x 33 cm)
The Gardens of the Zoological Society
of London map 33 ¹⁄₁₀ X 46 ⅔ in. (84 x 118.9 cm)
Penny Dreadful (Showtime Networks, 2014)
Production Designer: Jonathan McKinstry
Set Decorator: Philip Murphy
Art Director: Colman Corish
Graphic Designer: Annie Atkins
Sign Painter: Laurence O Toole
Courtesy of Showtime Networks Inc.

CHAPTER 2

POESIEALBUM
cover 8 x 5 in. (20.3 x 13 cm)
Photograph by Flora Fricker
Collection of Annie Atkins

PRINTED EPHEMERA
various sizes
Photograph by Flora Fricker
Collection of Annie Atkins

WHITE FIVER FRONT AND BACK
4¹⁄₁₀ x 7⅜ in. (12 x 19.5 cm)
Photograph by Flora Fricker
Collection of Annie Atkins

GOODS INVOICE: FABRIC DYING COMPANY
(Manchester, England, 1936)
7 x 8 in. (17.8 x 20.3 cm)
Photograph by Flora Fricker
Collection of Annie Atkins

SELECTION OF OBSERVER POCKET BOOKS
(England, 1937-c. 1960)
each 5½ x 3½ in. (14 x 8.9 cm)
Photograph by Flora Fricker
Collection of Annie Atkins

TELEGRAM (ENGLAND, 1941)
5 x 8 in. (12.7 x 20.3 cm)
Photograph by Flora Fricker
Collection of Annie Atkins

MILK-BOTTLE TOPS (ENGLAND, 1950s)
1½ in. (3.8 cm) diameter
Photograph by Flora Fricker
Collection of Annie Atkins

DEED WRITTEN ON VELLUM (ENGLAND, 1813)
15 x 24 in. (38 x 61 cm)
Photograph by Flora Fricker
Collection of Annie Atkins

CHALLENGE: A HANDWRITTEN MANUSCRIPT
BY VITA SACKVILLE-WEST
12½ x 8 in. (31.75 x 20.3 cm)
Photograph by Flora Fricker
Reprinted with kind permission of the
Dobkin Family Collection of Feminism

CINEMA TICKETS (CAIRO, EGYPT, EARLY 1940s)
2¼ x 3½ in. (5.7 x 8.9 cm)
Photograph by Flora Fricker
Collection of Annie Atkins

THE RMS TITANIC WITH FOUR WORKING FUNNELS
18 x 72 in. (45.7 x 183 cm)
Titanic: Blood and Steel (dir. Ciaran
Donnelly, 2012)
Production Designer: Tom Conroy
Art Director: Colman Corish
Set Decorator: Jil Turner
Graphic Designer: Annie Atkins
Photograph by Flora Fricker
Two drawings of The RMS Lusitania (fore
and aft) adapted and reprinted with kind
permission of the National Records of
Scotland and University of Glasgow Archives &
Special Collections, Upper Clyde Shipbuilders
collection, GB 248 UCS 1/110/367/20
Courtesy of Epos Films Ltd.

SKETCHES FOR SCIENCE FICTION ICONOGRAPHY
11 x 8½ in. (28 x 21.6 cm)
Annie Atkins's studio

CHAPTER 3

LETTERING SKETCHES FOR HOTEL SIGNAGE
11½ x 8 in. (29.2 x 20.3 cm)
The Grand Budapest Hotel (dir.
Wes Anderson, 2014)
Production Designer: Adam Stockhausen
Set Decorator: Anna Pinnock
Supervising Art Director: Gerald Sullivan
Art Director: Stephan O. Gessler
Graphic Designer: Annie Atkins
"THE GRAND BUDAPEST HOTEL" © 2014 Twentieth
Century Fox. All rights reserved.

THE MENDL'S BOX
5 x 5 x 5 in. (13 x 13 x 13 cm)
The Grand Budapest Hotel (dir.
Wes Anderson, 2014)
Production Designer: Adam Stockhausen
Set Decorator: Anna Pinnock
Property Master: Robin L. Miller
Graphic Designers: Annie Atkins &
Liliana Lambriev
Additional illustration: Jan Jericho
Photograph by Flora Fricker
"THE GRAND BUDAPEST HOTEL" © 2014 Twentieth
Century Fox. All rights reserved.

THREE KLUBECK BANKNOTES
largest 5 x 7½ in. (12.7 x 19 cm)
The Grand Budapest Hotel (dir.
Wes Anderson, 2014)
Production Designer: Adam Stockhausen
Set Decorator: Anna Pinnock
Property Master: Robin L. Miller

Graphic Designers: Annie Atkins &
Liliana Lambriev
Additional illustration: Miguel Schmid
Photograph by Flora Fricker
"THE GRAND BUDAPEST HOTEL" © 2014 Twentieth
Century Fox. All rights reserved.

ZUBROWKAN POSTAGE STAMPS
sheet 11½ x 8 in. (29.2 x 20.3 cm);
stamp 1³⁄₁₀ x 1 in. (3.3 x 2.5 cm)
The Grand Budapest Hotel (dir.
Wes Anderson, 2014)
Production Designer: Adam Stockhausen
Set Decorator: Anna Pinnock
Graphic Designers: Annie Atkins &
Liliana Lambriev
Illustration: Jan Jericho & Miguel Schmid
Photograph by Flora Fricker
"THE GRAND BUDAPEST HOTEL" © 2014 Twentieth
Century Fox. All rights reserved.

LUDWIG'S PRISON ESCAPE MAP
unfolded 18½ x 16 in. (47 x 40.6 cm)
The Grand Budapest Hotel (dir.
Wes Anderson, 2014)
Production Designer: Adam Stockhausen
Set Decorator: Anna Pinnock
Property Master: Robin L. Miller
Graphic Designers: Annie Atkins &
Liliana Lambriev
Additional illustration: Miguel Schmid &
Jan Jericho
Photograph by Flora Fricker
"THE GRAND BUDAPEST HOTEL" © 2014 Twentieth
Century Fox. All rights reserved.

SKETCHES FOR KEY FOB DESIGNS
11½ x 8 in. (29.2 x 20.3 cm)
The Grand Budapest Hotel (dir.
Wes Anderson, 2014)
Production Designer: Adam Stockhausen
Set Decorator: Anna Pinnock
Property Master: Robin L. Miller
Graphic Designer: Annie Atkins
Photograph by Flora Fricker
"THE GRAND BUDAPEST HOTEL" © 2014
Twentieth Century Fox. All rights reserved.

LUGGAGE TAGS
approx. 3 in. wide (7.6 cm wide)
The Grand Budapest Hotel (dir.
Wes Anderson, 2014)
Production Designer: Adam Stockhausen
Set Decorator: Anna Pinnock
Property Master: Robin L. Miller
Graphic Designers: Annie Atkins &
Liliana Lambriev
Photograph by Flora Fricker
"THE GRAND BUDAPEST HOTEL" © 2014 Twentieth
Century Fox. All rights reserved.

1960s RESTAURANT MENU
12½ x 8 in. (30.5 x 20.3 cm)

The Grand Budapest Hotel (dir.
Wes Anderson, 2014)
Production Designer: Adam Stockhausen
Set Decorator: Anna Pinnock
Property Master: Robin L. Miller
Graphic Designers: Annie Atkins &
Liliana Lambriev
Illustrator: Mary Heneghan
Calligrapher: Jan Jericho
Photograph by Flora Fricker
"THE GRAND BUDAPEST HOTEL" © 2014 Twentieth
Century Fox. All rights reserved.

GUSTAVE'S DEPOSITION
8 x 5½ in. (20.3 x 14 cm)
The Grand Budapest Hotel (dir.
Wes Anderson, 2014)
Production Designer: Adam Stockhausen
Set Decorator: Anna Pinnock
Property Master: Robin L. Miller
Graphic Designers: Annie Atkins &
Liliana Lambriev
Additional illustration: Miguel Schmid
Photograph by Flora Fricker
"THE GRAND BUDAPEST HOTEL" © 2014 Twentieth
Century Fox. All rights reserved.

THE LAST WILL AND TESTAMENT OF MADAME D.
15 x 9 in. (38.1 x 22.9 cm)
The Grand Budapest Hotel (dir.
Wes Anderson, 2014)
Production Designer: Adam Stockhausen
Set Decorator: Anna Pinnock
Property Master: Robin L. Miller
Graphic Designers: Annie Atkins &
Liliana Lambriev
Photograph by Flora Fricker
"THE GRAND BUDAPEST HOTEL" © 2014 Twentieth
Century Fox. All rights reserved.

MADAME D.'S NOTE TO GUSTAVE
8 x 6 in. (20.3 x 15.2 cm)
The Grand Budapest Hotel (dir.
Wes Anderson, 2014)
Production Designer: Adam Stockhausen
Set Decorator: Anna Pinnock
Property Master: Robin L. Miller
Graphic Designers: Annie Atkins &
Liliana Lambriev
Art Department Assistant: Molly Rosenblatt
Photograph by Flora Fricker
"THE GRAND BUDAPEST HOTEL" © 2014 Twentieth
Century Fox. All rights reserved.

BOOK OF ROMANTIC POETRY, VOL. I
8 x 5 in. (20.3 x 12.7 cm)
The Grand Budapest Hotel (dir.
Wes Anderson, 2014)
Production Designer: Adam Stockhausen
Set Decorator: Anna Pinnock
Property Master: Robin L. Miller
Graphic Designers: Annie Atkins &
Liliana Lambriev

Photograph by Flora Fricker
"THE GRAND BUDAPEST HOTEL" © 2014 Twentieth
Century Fox. All rights reserved.

JOPLING'S CALLING CARD
2 x 3½ in. (5.1 x 8.9 cm)
The Grand Budapest Hotel (dir.
Wes Anderson, 2014)
Production Designer: Adam Stockhausen
Set Decorator: Anna Pinnock
Property Master: Robin L. Miller
Graphic Designers: Annie Atkins &
Liliana Lambriev
Art Department Assistant: Miguel Schmid
Photograph by Flora Fricker
"THE GRAND BUDAPEST HOTEL" © 2014 Twentieth
Century Fox. All rights reserved.

TRANS-ALPINE YODEL
9½ x 12½ in. (24.1 x 31.8 cm)
The Grand Budapest Hotel (dir.
Wes Anderson, 2014)
Production Designer: Adam Stockhausen
Set Decorator: Anna Pinnock
Property Master: Robin L. Miller
Graphic Designers: Annie Atkins &
Liliana Lambriev
Photograph by Flora Fricker
"THE GRAND BUDAPEST HOTEL" © 2014 Twentieth
Century Fox. All rights reserved.

PRESS POSTERS
21 x 15 in. (53.3 x 38.1 cm)
The Grand Budapest Hotel (dir.
Wes Anderson, 2014)
Production Designer: Adam Stockhausen
Set Decorator: Anna Pinnock
Property Master: Robin L. Miller
Graphic Designer: Annie Atkins
Photographs by Flora Fricker
"THE GRAND BUDAPEST HOTEL" © 2014 Twentieth
Century Fox. All rights reserved.

POLICE REPORT
9½ x 8 in. (24.1 x 20.3 cm)
The Grand Budapest Hotel (dir.
Wes Anderson, 2014)
Production Designer: Adam Stockhausen
Set Decorator: Anna Pinnock
Property Master: Robin L. Miller
Graphic Designers: Annie Atkins &
Liliana Lambriev
Photograph of Jeff Goldblum as Deputy
Kovacs by Martin Scali
Photograph of prop by Flora Fricker
"THE GRAND BUDAPEST HOTEL" © 2014 Twentieth
Century Fox. All rights reserved.

THE GRAND BUDAPEST HOTEL BOOK
8 x 5 in. (20.3 x 12.7 cm)
The Grand Budapest Hotel (dir.
Wes Anderson, 2014)
Production Designer: Adam Stockhausen

Set Decorator: Anna Pinnock
Property Master: Robin L. Miller
Graphic Designers: Annie Atkins &
Liliana Lambriev
Photograph by Flora Fricker
"THE GRAND BUDAPEST HOTEL" © 2014 Twentieth
Century Fox. All rights reserved.

CHAPTER 4

FORTY-NINE TICKETS
1 x 2 in. (2.5 x 5 cm)
Photograph by Flora Fricker
Annie Atkins's studio

TWELVE YELLOW TELEGRAMS
4½ x 6 in. (11.4 x 15.2 cm)
The Grand Budapest Hotel (dir. Wes
Anderson, 2014)
Production Designer: Adam Stockhausen
Set Decorator: Anna Pinnock
Property Master: Robin L. Miller
Graphic Designers: Annie Atkins &
Liliana Lambriev
Photograph by Flora Fricker
"THE GRAND BUDAPEST HOTEL" © 2014 Twentieth
Century Fox. All rights reserved.

MULTICOLOR SCRIPT PAGES FROM THE SHREDDER
AT THE END OF A SHOOT
each page 11¾ x 8⅓ in. (29.7 x 21 cm)
Photograph by Flora Fricker

LOVE LETTERS: CONTINUITY REPEATS
3 x 5 in. (7.6 x 12.7 cm)
The Tudors (Showtime Networks, 2008)
Production Designer: Tom Conroy
Set Decorator: Crispian Sallis
Graphic Designer: Annie Atkins
Photograph by Megan K. Jones
Courtesy of TM Productions Ltd.

SKETCHES OF TWO US FLAGS
11 x 8½ in. (28 x 21.6 cm)
Annie Atkins's studio

EIGHT COFFEE STAINS
7 x 4 in. (17.8 x 10.1 cm)
Photograph by Mairead Lambert
Collection of Annie Atkins

FOURTEEN ENVELOPES
each 4 x 6½ in. (11.4 x 15.2 cm)
Vita & Virginia (dir. Chanya Button, 2017)
Production Designer: Noam Piper
Art Director: Neill Treacy
Graphic Designers: Felix McGinley &
Annie Atkins
Calligrapher: Sarah O'Dea
Photograph by Flora Fricker
Courtesy of Blinder Films

TWELVE MIX TAPES
3 x 4 in. (7.6 x 10.2 cm)
Photograph by Ailsa Williams
Collection of Annie Atkins

CHAPTER 5

"STEWED EELS & MASHED POTATOES:
ALWAYS READY" ARCHIVAL PHOTOGRAPH
Courtesy of Heritage England/London
Metropolitan Archives

SKETCH FOR SIGNAGE
11½ x 8 in. (29.2 x 20.3 cm)
Penny Dreadful (Showtime Networks, 2014)
Production Designer: Jonathan McKinstry
Graphic Designer: Annie Atkins
Photograph by Flora Fricker
Courtesy of Showtime Networks Inc.
and Annie Atkins studio

STREET POSTER: CHOLERA!
10½ x 8 in. (26.7 x 20.3 cm)
Grand Guignol theater frontage
Penny Dreadful (Showtime Networks, 2014)
Production Designer: Jonathan McKinstry
Graphic Designer: Annie Atkins
Photograph by Flora Fricker
Courtesy of Showtime Networks Inc.

SKETCH FOR DENTIST'S SIGN
11½ x 8 in. (29.2 x 20.3 cm)
Penny Dreadful (Showtime Networks, 2014)
Production Designer: Jonathan McKinstry
Graphic Designer: Annie Atkins
Courtesy of Showtime Networks Inc.
and Annie Atkins studio

SKETCH FOR UNDERTAKER'S SIGN
11½ x 8 in. (29.2 x 20.3 cm)
Penny Dreadful (Showtime Networks, 2014)
Production Designer: Jonathan McKinstry
Graphic Designer: Annie Atkins
Courtesy of Showtime Networks Inc.
and Annie Atkins studio

HOW TO WRITE TELEGRAMS PROPERLY
6 x 4 in. (15.2 x 10.2 cm)
Titanic: Blood and Steel (2012)
Production Designer: Tom Conroy
Set Decorator: Jil Turner
Graphic Designer: Annie Atkins
Photograph by Flora Fricker
Courtesy of Epos Films Ltd.

TITANIC MENUS
large 7⅓ x 5 in. (18.3 x 12.7);
small 5½ x 3½ in. (14 x 8.9 cm)
Titanic: Blood and Steel (2012)
Production Designer: Tom Conroy
Set Decorator: Jil Turner

Graphic Designer: Annie Atkins
Photograph by Flora Fricker
Courtesy of Epos Films Ltd.

SKETCH FOR PAWNBROKER'S SHOP WINDOW
11½ x 8 in. (29.2 x 20.3 cm)
Penny Dreadful (Showtime Networks, 2014)
Production Designer: Jonathan McKinstry
Graphic Designer: Annie Atkins
Courtesy of Showtime Networks Inc.
and Annie Atkins studio

NEW YORK SUBWAY SIGNS
various sizes
Bridge of Spies (dir. Steven Spielberg, 2015)
Production Designer: Adam Stockhausen
Supervising Art Director: Kim Jennings
Graphic Designer: Annie Atkins
"BRIDGE OF SPIES" © 2015 Twentieth Century
Fox. All rights reserved. Courtesy
of Storyteller Distribution Co., LLC.

SKETCH FOR GUNMAKER'S SIGN
11½ x 8 in. (29.2 x 20.3 cm)
Penny Dreadful (Showtime Networks, 2014)
Production Designer: Jonathan McKinstry
Graphic Designer: Annie Atkins
Courtesy of Showtime Networks Inc.
and Annie Atkins studio

STREET POSTER: THE MATCHGIRL'S STRIKE
10½ x 8 in. (26.7 x 20.3 cm)
Penny Dreadful (Showtime Networks, 2014)
Production Designer: Jonathan McKinstry
Graphic Designer: Annie Atkins
Photograph by Flora Fricker
Courtesy of Showtime Networks Inc.

BACKSTAGE SIGN
13 x 12 in. (33 x 30.5 cm)
Penny Dreadful (Showtime Networks, 2014)
Production Designer: Jonathan McKinstry
Graphic Designer: Annie Atkins
Sign Painter: Laurence O Toole
Photograph by Flora Fricker
Courtesy of Showtime Networks Inc.

THEATER SIGN
11½ x 8 in. (29.2 x 20.3 cm)
Penny Dreadful (Showtime Networks, 2014)
Production Designer: Jonathan McKinstry
Graphic Designer: Annie Atkins
Courtesy of Showtime Networks Inc.
and Annie Atkins studio

HOTEL MATCHBOX & STATIONERY
vintage US letter 10½ x 8 in.
(26.7 x 20.3 cm)
matchbox 1 ⅓ x 2 in (3.4 x 5 cm)
Bridge of Spies (dir. Steven Spielberg, 2015)
Production Designer: Adam Stockhausen
Set Decorator: Rena DeAngelo
Graphic Designer: Annie Atkins

Photograph by Flora Fricker
"BRIDGE OF SPIES" © 2015 Twentieth Century
Fox. All rights reserved. Courtesy
of Storyteller Distribution Co., LLC.

STREET SIGNAGE
various sizes, 2-6 ft. high (.6-1.8 m)
Bridge of Spies (dir. Steven Spielberg, 2015)
Production Designer: Adam Stockhausen
Supervising Art Director: Kim Jennings
Graphic Designer: Annie Atkins
"BRIDGE OF SPIES" © 2015 Twentieth Century
Fox. All rights reserved. Courtesy
of Storyteller Distribution Co., LLC.

CAFÉ MENU
20 x 10 in. (50.8 x 25.4 cm)
Penny Dreadful (Showtime Networks, 2014)
Production Designer: Jonathan McKinstry
Graphic Designer: Annie Atkins
Photograph by Flora Fricker
Courtesy of Showtime Networks Inc.

SKETCHES FOR JAPANESE CHARACTERS
11½ x 8 in. (29.2 x 20.3 cm)
Isle of Dogs (dir. Wes Anderson, 2018)
Production Designers: Paul Harrod &
Adam Stockhausen
Art Director: Curt Enderle
Graphic Designers: Erica Dorn & Annie Atkins
"ISLE OF DOGS" © 2018 Twentieth Century
Fox. All rights reserved.

CHAPTER 6

THREADS AND RIBBONS
Photograph by Flora Fricker
Collection of Annie Atkins

CHAPUYS'S LETTER
14 x 10 in. (35.6 x 25.4 cm)
The Tudors (Showtime Networks, 2008)
Production Designer: Tom Conroy
Set Decorator: Crispian Sallis
Graphic Designer: Annie Atkins
Calligrapher: Gareth Colgan
Photograph by Flora Fricker
Courtesy of TM Productions Ltd.

TUDOR COLLECTION
largest manuscript for scale 18 x 36 in.
(45.7 x 91.4 cm)
The Tudors (Showtime Networks, 2008)
Production Designer: Tom Conroy
Set Decorator: Crispian Sallis
Graphic Designer: Annie Atkins
Photograph by Flora Fricker
Courtesy of TM Productions Ltd.

KATHERINE HOWARD'S LETTER
5 x 3½ in. (12.7 x 8.9 cm)

The Tudors (Showtime Networks, 2008)
Production Designer: Tom Conroy
Set Decorator: Crispian Sallis
Graphic Designer: Annie Atkins
Calligrapher: Megan Breslin
Photograph by Flora Fricker
Courtesy of TM Productions Ltd.

HENRY VIII'S LIST OF POTENTIAL SUITORS
14 x 4½ in. (35.6 x 11.4 cm)
The Tudors (Showtime Networks, 2008)
Production Designer: Tom Conroy
Set Decorator: Crispian Sallis
Graphic Designer: Annie Atkins
Calligrapher: Gareth Colgan
Photograph by Flora Fricker
Courtesy of TM Productions Ltd.

STAINING AND AGING PAPER
Photographs by Flora Fricker
Collection of Annie Atkins

TEA-STAINING RECIPES
Photographs by Flora Fricker
Collection of Annie Atkins

FAKE BLOOD
Photograph by Flora Fricker
Collection of Annie Atkins

BASIC KIT
Photograph by Flora Fricker
Collection of Annie Atkins

PINK MEASURING TAPE
Photograph by Flora Fricker
Collection of Annie Atkins

TEENAGE DIARY
7 x 5 in. (17.8 x 12.7 cm)
Metal Heart (Dir. Hugh O'Conor, 2018)
Production Designer: Neill Treacy
Graphic Designer: Annie Atkins
Photograph by Flora Fricker
Courtesy of Rubicon Films

PAPER FASTENINGS
Photograph by Flora Fricker
Collection of Annie Atkins

GRAND GUIGNOL THEATER FRONTAGE
theater front 16 ft. wide (4.9 m)
Penny Dreadful (Showtime Networks, 2014)
Production Designer: Jonathan McKinstry
Supervising Art Director: Adam O'Neill
Graphic Designer: Annie Atkins
Sign Painters: Laurence O Toole &
Kenneth Carroll
Courtesy of Showtime Networks Inc.

EMBOSSING TAPE LETTERING
Photograph by Flora Fricker
Collection of Annie Atkins

ATARI'S STENCILED EMBLEM
8⅜ x 6 in. wide (21.3 x 15.2 cm)
Isle of Dogs (dir. Wes Anderson, 2018)
Production Designers: Paul Harrod &
Adam Stockhausen
Graphic Designers: Erica Dorn & Annie Atkins
"ISLE OF DOGS" © 2018 Twentieth Century
Fox. All rights reserved.

VARIOUS RUBBER STAMPS
approx. 1-2 in. (2.5-5 cm)
Photograph by Flora Fricker
Collection of Annie Atkins

LINOCUT LETTERS FOR THE TRASH ISLAND
DECREE
each letter 2 x 2 in. (5 x 5 cm)
Isle of Dogs (dir. Wes Anderson, 2018)
Production Designers: Paul Harrod &
Adam Stockhausen
Graphic Designers: Erica Dorn & Annie Atkins
Photograph by Flora Fricker
"ISLE OF DOGS" © 2018 Twentieth Century
Fox. All rights reserved.

DRY-TRANSFER LETTERING
Photograph by Flora Fricker
Collection of Annie Atkins

THREE TYPEWRITERS
OLIVETTI VALENTINE (1968)
Photograph by Bruce Atkins
Collection of John Gloyne

OLIVETTI DORA (1974)
Photograph by Flora Fricker
Collection of Annie Atkins

FACIT TP2 (1968)
Photograph by Flora Fricker
Collection of Dympna Treacy

BLANK ANTIQUE PAPER
(various sizes)
Photograph by Flora Fricker
Collection of Annie Atkins

ACKNOWLEDGMENTS

For Neill & Mabon Treacy.

I started a proposal for this book when I was pregnant with my baby and I finished the final edits a month after his third birthday. It's really only thanks to my parents-in-law, Tadhg and Dympna Treacy, that I managed to write this at all: knowing that he was loved and happy while I stole some hours to work meant everything, and this book wouldn't have happened without them. Thank you!

To all the people who passed through my studio while I was writing: Megan Breslin, Flavia Ballarin, Gregory Cullen, Karen Kenny, Jules Gawlik, Laurine Cornuéjols, Lucie Wolfe, Lucy McCullough, Joel Proudfoot, Mabel Dilliway, Rachael McCabe, Megan Jones, Luís Calvário, Samuel Tomé, Rose Montgomery, and Katy Galvin—your input is evident in every chapter of this book, thank you for all your hard work in making this come together. Thanks also to James Kelleher, Regan Hutchins, Kevin Donovan, Clare Bell, Mary Ann Bolger, and Valgeir Valdimarsson for their wisdom, and my special thanks to Ailsa Williams and Alan Lambert, whose contributions to this book have been so valuable to me, and who make my studio a more creative place every day. My extra special thanks goes to Mairead Lambert, who was nothing short of brilliant in both her eagle-eyed work on the book itself and in juggling so much artwork in the studio while I had my head buried in the manuscript.

I'd also like to thank some of my colleagues in filmmaking around the world for the insight and memories that they shared with me for these pages: the graphic designer Liliana Lambriev; the prop man Till Sennhenn; the art directors Irene O'Brien and Colman Corish; the set decorators George DeTitta, Susan Bode-Tyson, and Anna Pinnock; and the property masters Robin Miller, Eckart Friz, and Sandy Hamilton. A very special thanks to Adam Stockhausen, Wes Anderson, and Jeremy Dawson: working on The Grand Budapest Hotel was a life-changing experience. Not a day goes by that I don't thank my lucky stars for being able to contribute something to such a beautiful film, and I'm thrilled to be able to share some of the artwork on these pages. I'd also like to thank the production designer Tom Conroy for giving me my start in filmmaking, when I was a quite young and very green film graduate; the brilliant Pilar Valencia for teaching me so much about the craft; and the set decorator Crispian Sallis for instilling in me an eye for detail. My heartfelt thanks also to Bjarni Einarsson, Nelson Lowry, and Fiona McCann for their respective leg ups.

To Sara Bader, my brilliant editor, thank you so much for making this book happen, for all your expertise, and for keeping it on the right track throughout its creation. My thanks also to Deb Aaronson, the book's publisher, who championed the idea from the very beginning, and to Meagan Bennett, the book's artworker, who puzzled it all together so beautifully. And to Julia Hasting, for the book's wonderfully cool design concept, thank you for choosing Courier Sans: it's the last font I would have ever considered and it's absolutely perfect. Thanks also to the copy editor Linda Lee, the proofreader Tanya Heinrich, the clearance coordinator Paula Byrden, and the production controller Sarah Kramer for their vigilance. To Flora Fricker, the book's photographer, thank you for all the beautiful pictures, and for also being a fantastic prop-maker, graphic designer, and stylist in the process.

Finally to my parents, Mary Heneghan and Bruce Atkins, for being my original design mentors. This book was written largely in memory of their friend, the artist Peter Prendergast, whose philosophies on the creative process have always stayed with me.

Phaidon Press Limited
Regent's Wharf
All Saints Street
London N1 9PA

Phaidon Press Inc.
65 Bleecker Street
New York, NY 10012

phaidon.com

First published 2020
© 2020 Phaidon Press Limited

ISBN 978 0 7148 7938 3

A CIP catalogue record for
this book is available from
the British Library and the
Library of Congress.

All rights reserved. No part
of this publication may be
reproduced, stored in a
retrieval system or transmitted,
in any form or by any means,
electronic, mechanical,
photocopying, recording
or otherwise, without the
written permission of
Phaidon Press Limited.

Commissioning Editor: Sara Bader
Project Editor: Sara Bader
Production Controller: Sarah Kramer
Jacket and cover: Annie Atkins
Design: Julia Hasting
Artworker: Meagan Bennett

Printed in China

740.92
A367f

ATK

This book wouldn't have been possible
without the people who helped make it.

Date	Name
Jan 30 '18	Flavia Ballarin
JAN 31 '18	GREGORY CULLEY
FEB 1 '18	Karen Fenny
Feb 25 '18	Mairéad Lambert
MAR 13 '18	Jules Gawlik
Apr 20 '18	Laurine Cornuéjols
May 17 '18	Lucie Wolfe
May 21 '18	Lucy McCullough
Jun 9 '18	AILSA WILLIAMS
Jul 22 '18	Mabel Alliway
Aug 5 '18	Flora Fricker
Aug 10 '18	Rachael McCabe
Aug 11 '18	Megan Jones
Nov 27 '18	Katy Galvin
JAN 26 '19	Rose Montgomery
MAR 13 '19	Jim Gregory
JUN 11 19	Luis Calvário
JUL 7 19	Samuel Tomé
JUL 17 19	JOEL PROUDFOOT